QUILTS
from two
VALLEYS

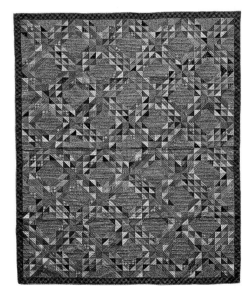

Flower Basket, *the Shenandoah Valley (VA), c. 1940, cotton, 77 x 88, made by Wilda Brunk Showalter (a member of the Old Order Mennonites) for one of her 26 grandchildren, owned by Brian and Martha Shank.*

   The Flower Baskets in this pattern, an old Valley favorite, were pieced by hand. Wilda made all the baskets and petals of a single, plain green fabric, filled each basket with a print fabric, and then finished each block with a third fabric. The green acts as a neutral color, steadying the busyness around it.
   The solid peach blocks show off their quilting, yet do not challenge the fine piecing or choice of fabrics in the Basket blocks.

QUILTS
from two
VALLEYS

Amish Quilts from the Big Valley,
Mennonite Quilts from the Shenandoah Valley

Phyllis Pellman Good

Good Books
Intercourse, PA 17534
800/762-7171

Acknowledgments and Credits

This project benefited from the goodwill, generosity, and knowledge of many people. I owe particular thanks to: Connie Hayes, Big Valley quilt scholar; The Virginia Quilt Museum, The Virginia Quilt Research Project, and Joan Knight, Director of the Museum and the Project; Scott Suter, Curator of the Shenandoah Valley Folk Art and Heritage Center; Lois Bowman and Harold Huber of the Menno Simons Historical Library, Eastern Mennonite University; all owners who graciously loaned their quilts and artifacts, and spent significant time telling me about particlar quiltmakers and quiltmaking traditions; my husband, Merle, who helped to conceive this project and helped at many knotty points along the way.

Photography credits—Jerry Irwin: front cover (woman with child), pages 7 (top), 19 (bottom), 20 (top), 25 (top), 32 (top and center); Dick Brown: pages 8 (top), 9 (top), 43; Stephen Scott: page 32 (bottom); Lucian Niemeyer: page 47 (top); Ken Layman: pages 48 (top), 49, 73; Samuel Horst and Western Reserve Historical Society, Cleveland, OH: page 56.
All quilts photographed by Paul Jacobs except pages 2, 6, 9, 34. Those quilt photographs are courtesy of David Wheatcroft.

"Green Market, New York" by Julia Kasdorf first appeared in *Festival Quarterly*, Fall 1989.

Design by Dawn J. Ranck

Library of Congress Cataloging-in-Publication Data

Good, Phyllis Pellman
    Quilts from two valleys : Amish quilts from the Big Valley, Mennonite quilts from the
Shenandoah Valley / Phyllis Pellman Good.
        p. cm.
        Includes bibliographical references and index.
        ISBN 1-56148-286-2
        1. Quilts, Amish--Pennsylvania--Kishacoquillas Creek Region. 2. Quilts, Mennonite--
Shenandoah River Valley (Va., and W. Va.)
I. Title
NK9112.G66 1999
746.46'088'287--dc 21   99-36723
                                                                                                          CIP

Table of Contents

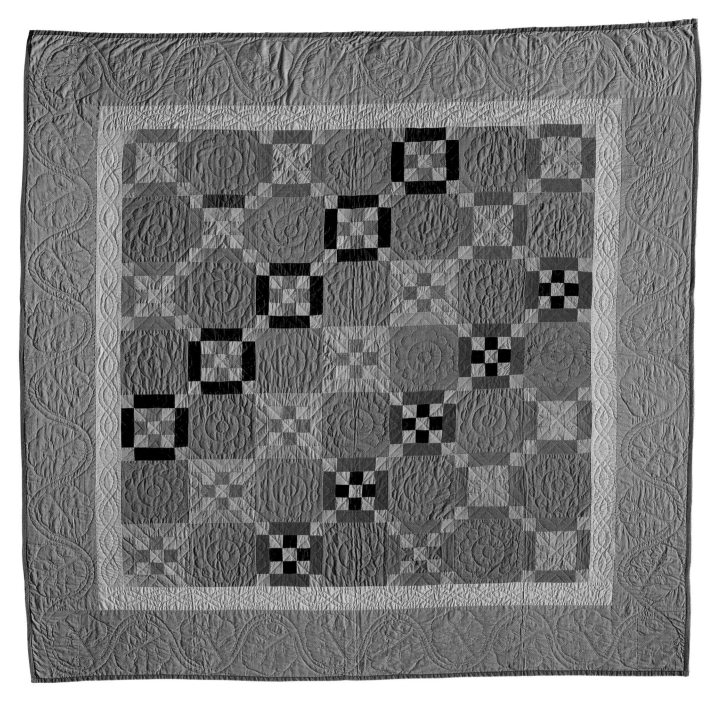

Double Nine-Patch Chain, *the Big Valley (PA), c. 1920-30, cotton percale, cotton/rayon, cotton sateen, photograph courtesy of David Wheatcroft.*

In this simply pieced quilt, the quiltmaker has set off several layers of activity. She has positioned the Nine-Patch blocks within larger squares with corner blocks. By consistently using pink for the corner blocks and for the alternating squares within each Nine-Patch, she has also created a Single Irish Chain pattern.

Simple, open-faced flowers are quilted on each solid green square, softening the crisp piecing. But each of those round blooms is surrounded by diagonal rows of straight quilting that follow the Irish Chain paths. That quilting subtly reinforces the diagonal movement across the quilt top and appears to bisect many of the small squares into triangles.

Stories of Two Valleys and Their Quilts

Two hidden valleys—the Big Valley in central Pennsylvania, the Shenandoah Valley in western Virginia—held vibrant communities and quilting traditions during the closing years of the 19th century and the early decades of the 20th century. These were the years when quilts made by the Amish and Mennonites were abundantly artistic. How did their quilts, made in these two tucked-away places, compare?

Making a quilt is usually a private undertaking. The quiltmaker chooses her own fabric and colors and piecing patterns; assembled into a quilt, they show her personal preferences, her cautions or derring-do. But in many cases that quilt also reflects the community in which the quiltmaker lives—the restrictions or encouragement of the local church, the influence of her neighbors, the visual vocabulary that she's learned from her family or the settlement from which they've emigrated. These forces certainly affected quiltmakers in both the Big and Shenandoah valleys.

Historic events also leave their mark on quiltmaking. For example, in central Pennsylvania and in western Virginia, the Industrial Revolution brought many new fabrics to the marketplace. Some quilted well; others didn't. The Civil War and Reconstruction interrupted life in many ways, including quilt production.

Although they are religious cousins, the Amish and Mennonites created quite different quilts during these years of peak quilt design. Who influenced their choice of patterns and fabrics and color combinations? What part did their churches play? How were these two particular communities affected by their separate histories, and by events in the larger world?

The Big Valley in Pennsylvania's Mifflin County was (and continues to be) home to three main Old Order Amish groups. While the three groups differ in their quilt traditions, most of the quilts made in the Valley share certain characteristics—they are made of solid-color-fabric (without prints); they are graphically strong and bold with occasional flashes of powerful color.

Precisely pieced but somewhat more subdued quilts were made at the same time by the Mennonites of the Shenandoah Valley. Their quilts are distinguished by their plentiful quilting, their minute stitches.

The Amish and Mennonite quilts in this book have also had quite different histories since the mid-1970s. Many Amish quilts made between 1880 and 1940 have become prized as pieces of art. Many Amish families were ready to trade their family bedcovers for cash. Now many of those quilts are owned by collectors who value them for their artistic beauty.

By contrast, most of the Mennonite quilts in this book are still within the families where they were made. Sometimes stored in chests, sometimes used on a bed, sometimes hung on a wall, these quilts continue to be passed from one generation to the next.

This book holds parts of the stories of 61 quilts—and parts of the communities' stories where they were made.

(on next page)

North Carolina Lily, *the Big Valley (PA), c. 1935-40, cotton, 74 x 94, maker belonged to "Black-Toppers" (Peachey/Renno Amish), private collection.*

The pieced blocks and the solid, quilted blocks balance each other well in their beauty and interest.
Deep resonant tones of color support, rather than compete with, the intricate quilting patterns. A leaf with well-defined veins in the outer border is a a variation of the beloved Big Valley mulberry leaf quilting theme.

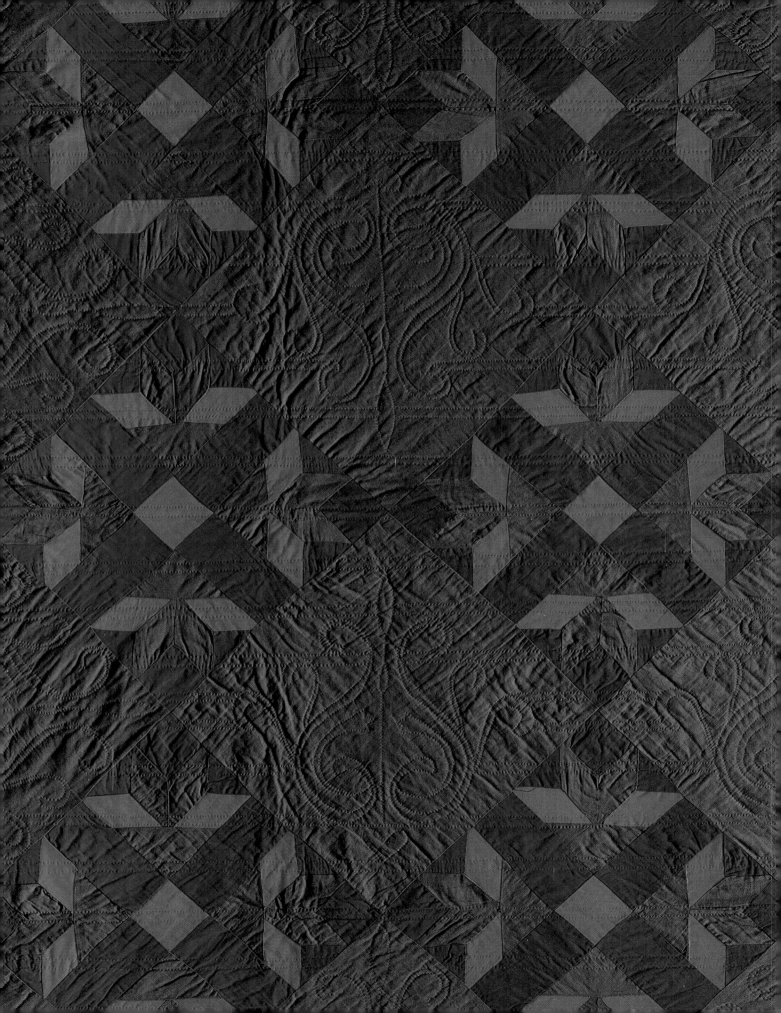

AMISH QUILTS
from the BIG VALLEY

The Amish of Pennsylvania's Big Valley

It is a quiet, slim valley, home to five main groups of Amish (among them, three Old Order groups) and as many kinds of Mennonites.

Amish have farmed the Big Valley for two centuries. There they have worked out what they believe—and how they ought to live as a result.

Their distinguishing clothing patterns reflect their effort to live faithfully. So do their colorful buggies: one

Nine-Patch, *the Big Valley (PA), c. 1935-45, plain- and twill-weave cotton, plain- and twill-weave cotton/rayon, 72½ x 81, photography courtesy of David Wheatcroft.*

This sea of squares seems to hover just above the blue background. Each pieced block is a Four-Patch in Nine-Patch, a relatively simple pattern that realizes a level of complexity because of the way color is used.

The interplay of black and tan squares creates the effect of rows of beads running both vertically and horizontally across the face of the quilt. Occasionally other colors are substituted, bringing movement of light to the pattern.

group drives buggies with white tops; another drives carriages with brilliant yellow tops; a third, buggies with black tops.

The Amish have found a vocabulary of images that announces their commitments. In this Valley in south-central Pennsylvania, even the condition of a farmstead and lawn shows which group the resident family belongs to—and what they value.

This is a world of visual language, drawn out daily along Back Mountain Road, Three Penny Lane, Maple Grove Road.

The quilts these people have made are a part of that language, in their pieced patterns, their color palettes, their quilting motifs. Made primarily as bedcovers, the early quilts from this Valley reveal a gentle beauty; they also show evidence of the churches' boundaries and of a people's strength.

Why Did the Amish Choose the Big Valley?

The time was the 1790s. Prompted partly by the spirit of the age (the first Amish pioneered in the New World in 1736) and partly by the lure of new farmland, several Amish families from Lancaster and Berks counties moved onto the limestone soil of the Valley. News of a particularly difficult encounter with native Americans in Berks County may have spurred them on, also.

They bought cleared land from Scots-Irish settlers who were already on the move out of the Valley.

The Big Valley is known formally as the Kishacoquillas Valley, named for the creek which runs along the base of Jacks Mountain. That ridge defines the south side of the Valley, Stone Mountain its northern border. Located in Mifflin County, the three- to four-mile-wide Valley lies at a southwest-northeast angle, about 30 miles in length.

The Yoders, Hooleys, Zooks, and Detweilers moved in between 1792 and 1805. By 1811, a tax list shows 56 Amish households to have been established, 51 of whom owned land and were classified as farmers.[1]

Amish homes of that period had few heirlooms. There was little extra time to make treasures, nor money to buy them. Furthermore, the Amish were cautious about possessions, especially those that didn't contribute directly to a well-functioning farm or to one's part in a sober religious community.

The Amish choose clothing and transportation that distinguish them from the larger world, yet they have continual exchange with persons from that world.

Church Life in the Big Valley, Mid-19th Century

As the Amish community grew and stretched through the Valley, it became impractical to function as a single church district with only one bishop. In the 1830s, the Valley was divided into three geographical sections so that leaders could perform more effectively.

When trouble developed in the Upper District and leaders from the Lower District got involved, a break in fellowship occurred between the churches.

The Lower District congregations eventually came to be nicknamed the "Bylers," after one of their significant leaders. They are still an identifiable group within the Big Valley, quickly distinguished by the bright yellow tops on their buggies. For that, they are routinely referred to as "Yellow-Toppers," an acceptable label within the community.

Ever concerned with living faithfully, the Amish have experienced numerous debates through the years as they encountered new realities or came upon new understandings of old teachings. A few years after the Byler group formed, leaders in the Middle District disagreed with leaders in the Upper District about the appropriate way to baptize new members. Despite enlisting counsel and assistance from beyond the Big Valley, the two groups eventually divided.

The larger group, whose leader came from the Middle District, joined with the Amish Mennonites—also known as the "Church Amish"—a more progressive movement taking shape in other Amish communities.

The smaller side in the baptism controversy came to be called the Peachey group, named, as was customary, for several of their leaders. Today the descendants of these people are called "Peacheys" or "Rennos," distinct from the Valley's other Amish because of several practices, including driving black-topped buggies. Consequently, they are usually called "Black-Toppers."

There were more disturbances among the "Old Church" (or Byler group) by the 1880s. A number of laypeople worried that the church was less committed than in former years, that they were drifting toward worldliness. Not able to gain the sympathy that they wanted from their official church leaders, they reached for support from Yost H. Yoder, a Mifflin County native who had gone to Nebraska to form a settlement in Gosper County. Yoder was reluctant to get involved

Range of Mountains, *the Big Valley (PA), c. 1925-30, cotton and sateen, 77 x 84, maker belonged to "Yellow-Toppers" (Byler Amish), private collection.*

Pairs of pieced pink and red triangles cut paths across this quilt from the Kanagy family. Where the diagonal channels cross, eight-patch pinwheels are formed, creating yet another kind of motion.

Quilted chevrons in the outer border echo the pieced triangles. Quilted single and multiple hearts, along with the bud image, soften the crisp lines of piecing.

A contemporary Nebraska Amish family displays their winter's work—and hopes for sales!

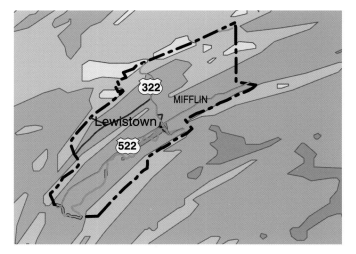

Mifflin County's Big Valley in the state of Pennsylvania.

because the inquiring group included no ordained leaders.

The conservative dissenters, not about to be deterred, persuaded an ordained deacon to join them. His criteria being met, Yoder came back to the Big Valley from Nebraska and ordained a bishop and a minister, thus establishing the group's credentials so it could be recognized as a new church. From the beginning, and continuing today, this group was known as the "Nebraska Amish." They are still the most conservative group of all Amish. Their clothing, their buildings, their white-topped buggies—and their quilts—set them clearly apart from their sister groups. They are often nicknamed, not surprisingly, "White-Toppers."

In the Big Valley by 1900, five main groups had sprung from the first Amish families who moved into the area about a century earlier. Three were Old Orders—the Bylers, the Nebraskas, and the Peacheys (known in more recent years as the Rennos). Two were "Church Amish."

Some further divisions occurred as time went on, but the three Amish groups that became distinctively identifiable by the closing decades of the 1800s are still the primary Amish fellowships in the Big Valley.

The Amish Begin to Make Quilts

The Amish came relatively late to quiltmaking. They may have considered it frivolous work. They may have also thought it impractical, since fine cottons and wools responded best to quilting, when many Amish families had flannels and ticking and muslin in their inventories instead.

But following the Civil War, industrialization increased, making a variety of high quality fabrics widely available at economical prices. There were more colors to select from. The weaves were more finely done. Patchwork quilts, while unknown among the Amish before 1880, began to appear after that time.[2] From then on, quiltmaking seemed to capture Amish women s attention and imagination.

Within the Amish community in general, life had begun to settle down. The tensions about how strictly

Despite their somber appearance, the Amish love color and design in their flowerbeds and in their quilts.

Plain Quilt, *the Big Valley (PA), 1849, cotton, photograph courtesy of David Wheatcroft.*

The earliest known, dated Amish quilt. The top is made of two large swaths of fabric, sewn together by hand with brown, handspun, cotton thread. The quilting creates the look of blocks, done in alternating motifs of stars and wreaths. The center medallion is embroidered with B.P., 1849.

The backing fabric was wrapped front to form the binding along the two sides. Yellow strips of cotton were handsewn to the top and bottom to form their bindings.

to follow the *Ordnung* (the agreed-upon standards which the Amish live by) began to find some resolution during the mid-1860s. Those more inclined to tradition took on a new identity as Old Orders, while those more comfortable with change began to affiliate with the Church Amish or Amish Mennonites.

That shift created clarity on many fronts. It may have even left its mark on quiltmaking, allowing those who wanted to be more experimental to do so, and setting clear expectations for those who preferred more defined boundaries.

Freedom to explore a functional art form coincided with the greater availability of pleasing fabric. At the same time, these women s sewing skills were still highly developed. In addition, they had few distractions for their creative energies.

No frown came from an artistic community dictating acceptable color combinations and piecing proportions. Beside economic and time restraints, an Amish quiltmaker knew only the restrictions of her church, who did discourage showing off and behaving excessively.

Quilting had found its place in this structured religious world that valued work, as well as church and family connections.

It is within these definitions, formulated by the church and enforced by the community s will, that the Amish women of the Big Valley made their quilts.

One-Patch Cross Grid, *the Big Valley (PA), c. 1925-30, cotton, 71 x 82, maker belonged to "White-Toppers" (Nebraska Amish), private collection.*

Despite her limited choice of patterns and colors, this quiltmaker produced a grid of softly modulated colors against—what appears to be—a black backdrop.

Working only with squares of two sizes, she "painted" a softly purple central lattice and hung slashes of light in each corner. The black blocks play a supportive part, not overwhelming the design.

Chain quilting runs through both borders. An extra strand is added to the wider outer borders.

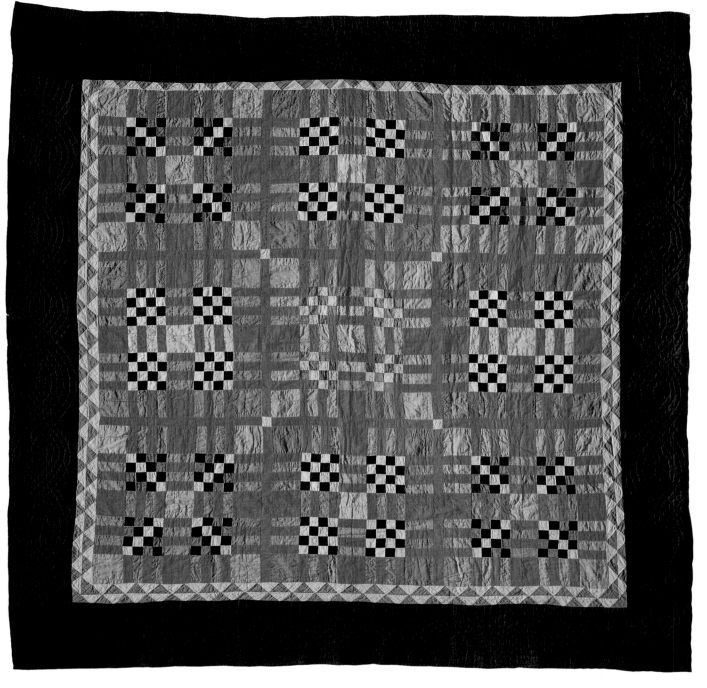

Four-Patch Variation, *the Big Valley (PA), c. 1935-40, cotton, 69 x 70, from the collection of Faith and Stephen Brown.*

The Four-Patch Variation rises to an unusual level of complexity in the overall arrangement of these 16-Patch (or Four-Patch-by-Four-Patch) blocks.

Rectangular red and blue pieces create a grid-like structure against which the highly-pieced square blocks float.

The layout of the little squares making up the large pieced blocks in the four corners creates strong diagonal motion.

But near the center of the quilt lie four yellow square blocks, providing a simple anchor to the organized activity.

The top border of pieced triangles is only one row wide, in contrast to the double rows on the other sides.

Erratic rows of quilting run through the pieced blocks. Orderly cables fill the outer border.

Cross and Four-Patch, *the Big Valley (PA), c. 1930-35, cotton, 73 x 82, maker belonged to "Yellow-Toppers" (Byler Amish), private collection.*

Neon pink and blue patches lie in formation against solid navy blocks and borders.

Each pieced block is composed of four pink and navy Four-Patches, held together by four blue rectangles and a pink center square.

The pink horizontal and vertical chains are unbroken, save for the bottom row, the third patch from the right. There, two Four-Patches were attached inconsistently, perhaps by choice, perhaps by accident.

Gentle wreath quilting fills the solid navy blocks.

Delectable Mountains, *the Big Valley (PA), c. 1920-30, plain-weave cotton and cotton sateen, 78 x 79, private collection.*

This combination of two pieced forms—triangles and squares—results in ever-enlarging, yet partially hidden, blocks and peaks.

The sawtooth inner border adds definition and a clear break between the sharp-edged piecing and the florid quilting in the outer border.

In this quilt the quilting is not an afterthought, but an integral element. The feathers and wreaths fit their spaces; the crosshatching extends the geometric action of the piecing.

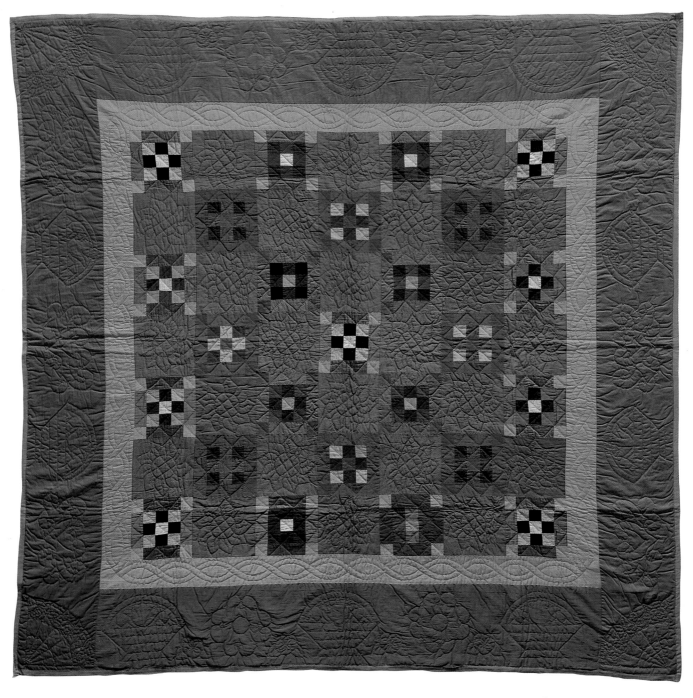

Nine-Patch in Blockwork, *the Big Valley (PA), c. 1935-40, 74 x 77, maker belonged to "Yellow-Toppers" (Byler Amish), private collection.*

Nine-Patch blocks, each sitting on their flat sides, each surrounded by a border of rectangles and corner blocks, form a unified pieced design.

This is a highly organized quilt. The pieced block in the center of the quilt, as well as those in the four corners, are exactly alike, color-wise.

Color continues to create this quilt's overall design as the pieced blocks move out in steps away from the center, and as they rest along the inner borders.

Sprucie Hearts, a favorite and distinctive quilting pattern in the Big Valley, alternate with quilted baskets in the side outer borders.

Double Nine-Patch, *the Big Valley (PA), c. 1930, cotton, cotton sateen back, 73 x 80, maker belonged to "White-Toppers" (Nebraska Amish), William and Connie Hayes.*

This wedding quilt was made for the groom, Jacob B. Hostetler (notice his initials embroidered in red near the bottom). It was most often the groom's quilts that carried the highest workmanship. Both a bride and groom brought quilts from their respective families to their marriage. Typically, the wife's were used first; the husband's were stashed away. Consequently, great care and imagination went into making sons' wedding quilts. In many cases, the quilts that survived are the best ones because they were never, or seldom, used.[3]

Made of men's and women's clothing fabrics (thus, the restricted use of colors), the quilt shows more planning than most made by Nebraska Amish.

Despite the fact that this is a special quilt, some of the little squares have been pieced, showing how hard it is to refuse the well-ingrained practice of salvaging and working with scraps.

What Distinguishes Big Valley Amish Quilts, Pre-1940?

Patterns and Designs

Big Valley Amish quiltmakers seemed to like piecing and designing more than quilting. (Their Lancaster "sisters" invested far more time and effort in intricately stitched, complex quilting patterns.)

Some patchwork designs that were beloved in the Lancaster community were also made in the Big Valley— Bars, and Sunshine and Shadow, for example. But in gen-

One-Patch Crib, *the Big Valley (PA), 1910, cotton, 48 x 49¹/₂, maker belonged to "White-Toppers" (Nebraska Amish), William and Connie Hayes.*

The off-center, pieced central area gives credence to the theory that Nebraska Amish women tried not to plan their quilts, thereby remaining free of pride and choosing to be industrious rather than imaginative.

This typical Nebraska Amish quilt was made for John J. Yoder by his mother. Yoder became a well-known bishop. (He was the nephew of Mose Yoder, one of the group who came from Nebraska to the Big Valley to help with the church troubles.)

The red blocks may have come from a dress Mrs. Yoder wore as a child and saved. Girls are permitted to wear red going-away or Sunday dresses.

eral, Mifflin County quilters were drawn to finer piecework. Four- and Nine-Patch variations abounded. Other favorite patterns were blockwork in many schemes: Irish Chain, Shoofly, Jacob's Ladder, Baskets, Tumbling Blocks, Log Cabin, and Crazy Patches.

With their interest and experimentation in patchwork, Big Valley Amish quilters found common ground with Amish quiltmakers in Ohio and further west. The Amish of Mifflin County chose to rear their families and cultivate their farms in a valley somewhat removed from the heavy traffic of the larger world. But they remained a way station for Amish migrations to Ohio and Nebraska, to Kansas and even North Dakota. Some pioneers returned, bringing what they had learned, leaving traces of scattered Amish settlements wherever they visited or finally chose to stay.

Quilt patterns traveled, too, often taking on details that identified them with a particular community, even if the basic design had originated elsewhere.

The Peacheys (Black-Toppers) took the greatest liberties with piecing designs and color choices. As members of the most change-minded of the three main Amish groups in the Valley, these women seemed to make quilts free of cautions from the church. The Peacheys maintained connections to the Amish church beyond Mifflin County, so they were continually exposed to practices in other communities.

The Byler group (Yellow-Toppers) tended to make more conservative quilts than the Peacheys, frequently choosing Blockwork and Four- and Nine-Patch designs. In that they reflect their more traditional leanings. Yet there are Byler quilts that display flair in both piecing and color. Although quite uniform, the group was not monolithic in practice. Districts could take on their own small but noticeable flavors, depending upon their leaders.

In quiltmaking, as with the rest of their lives, the Nebraskas (White-Toppers) lived with the greatest restrictions. Three basic piecing patterns were available to them—Nine-Patch, Four-Patch, and Blockwork. A nearly infinite number of variations of each of these designs was possible—creating a Double Four-Patch or Double Nine-Patch, setting the pieced blocks on point or on their flat sides, altering the sizes of individual patches within a Nine-Patch block, or working just with sin-

17

gle squares arranged randomly over the quilt top.

Each of these choices led to a particular overall effect when the blocks were assembled into a whole. Some quilts were carefully planned. Others appear to be purposely unorganized, as if the quilter had determined to make her project functional rather than aesthetic.

While these quiltmakers worked within clear limitations, their Four- and Nine-Patch options seemed to be enough; in fact, they seemed to be appropriate to their equally limited number of acceptable colors.

Nebraska quilts are modest and subdued. In that they mirror the choices of their makers, who live carefully attuned to both the natural world and the other members of their group.

Embroidery on Quilts

For many years, Nebraska women tended to label their quilts by embroidering two or three initials onto the tops.

Peachey women occasionally did more decorative embroidery as part of a quilt's design, often using fencerow or turkey track stitching on Crazy patches.[4]

Quilting Patterns in the Big Valley

Quilting styles and motifs can be guides in identifying Mifflin County quilts. In general, their quilting patterns are somewhat simpler and more abstract than those on Lancaster's quilts. They tend to be "flatter," less complex, and less graceful than Lancaster plumes, grapevines, and ferns.

Certain motifs were peculiar to the Big Valley. A vine of blackberry leaves appeared frequently on the borders of Byler quilts and occasionally on Nebraska ones.

A design known as the Sprucie Heart was used by all three Amish groups, often showing up on the solid blocks within the quilt top. Tulips on stems, a heart within a heart, pinwheels, and baskets were favorites especially of the Bylers and Peacheys.[5]

Even in quiltmaking there was room for tiny rebellions. One Nebraska bishop's daughter wanted to quilt baskets into the plain blocks of her quilt top. Her father urged her not to, and so she didn't. Instead she quilted a single basket over the entire quilt. It was such a large image one could easily miss seeing it![6]

The Peacheys, Bylers, and Nebraskas all did straight rows of quilting, often running on the diagonal over the entire top. Sometimes on older quilts, it was a double track of quilting; sometimes it was confined only to the border.

The Nebraskas were held primarily to two other border patterns—the chain and the fan. The chain could have between one and six strands, varying to accommodate the width of the border. A twist is a variation of the chain,

formed when the lines of intersecting loops are removed. Most women used tin or cardboard stencils to mark these patterns.

The height and width of a repeating fan pattern could be adjusted to fill a border area. A quiltmaker customarily marked the fans with a sliver of soap on the end of a string, eyeballing each loop in relation to the one just before it.[7]

Bindings on Big Valley Quilts

This very practical part of a quilt was handled very practically by Big Valley quilters. Most quilts were given relatively narrow bindings, usually from ¼ inch to one inch wide. (In that they resemble Ohio quilts more than Lancaster ones.)

Among the Nebraskas and Bylers it was a common practice to bring the quilt backing front to cover the

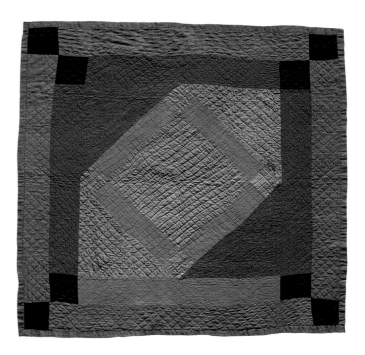

Center Diamond Crib, *the Big Valley (PA), c. 1940-45, cotton, 48 x 48, maker belonged to "White-Toppers" (Nebraska Amish), private collection.*

This quiltmaker worked with what she had. Despite its fabric imperfections (three sides of the inner border are purple; the fourth side is blue), the quilt has a degree of complexity. The border surrounding the center diamond, as well as the inner and outer borders, have corner blocks.

Notice the fade lines in the blue outer border. The fabric may have once been the pleated skirt of a dress, here recycled into a new use.

This quilt's colors are those typically used by the Nebraskas. That includes the brown binding which was formed by wrapping the quilt's backing front to finish the raw edges.

Cornshocks dot the fields that spread between the two ranges of mountains.

quilt's raw edges, or to wrap the quilt's border fabric around to the back and handstitch it in place to finish the edges. This was a plainer approach than choosing a separate or contrasting fabric for the binding.

The bindings on these quilts were frequently pieced and of different colors, because they were usually the backing fabrics, which themselves were often pieced. Sometimes this variety and placement of colors appears planned; many times it clearly was not.[8]

Fabric Changes Through the Years

With the industrialization that followed the Civil War, fabrics friendly to quilting became increasingly available. Amish women chose factory-made cottons and fine wools for their clothing and, consequently, for their quilts. They made some use also of flannels and suiting wool.

They shopped at local dry goods stores and from the Sears & Roebuck and Montgomery Ward catalogs. In some communities, peddlers visited Amish farms, stocked with the dry goods they knew these women wanted.

The Depression instigated a search for less expensive materials. Then World War II caused severe shortages of natural fibers. Newly "created" fabrics began coming on the market at reasonable prices and in intriguing colors.

In Lewistown, just over Jacks Mountain from the Big Valley, the American Viscose Company opened a factory in 1921. They made rayon and sold it in a nearby outlet where Amish women discovered its favorable price. It quilted well, also. Rayon began appearing in Mifflin County quilts in the 1920s and '30s (but only after 1940 in other communities).[9]

Polyesters and acrylics were quickly dubbed "miracle-fabrics" for their durability. Many buyers were drawn to their rainbow of pastel shades. But they brought an end to the tradition of richly colored quilts covered with fine stitching.

The new fibers did not absorb colors as intensely as the old. Nor did synthetic battings require as many stitches to anchor them in place as the traditional blankets and flannels demanded.

Blockwork, *the Big Valley (PA), c. 1880s, wool from men's suiting, 65 x 67½, maker belonged to "White-Toppers" (Nebraska Amish), William and Connie Hayes.*

This historic quilt traveled by buggy from Nebraska, back to Pennsylvania's Big Valley in the 1880s. In it was wrapped a little Yoder boy whose father had been called back to the Big Valley, away from his prairie homestead, to help settle trouble in the Amish church.

The transplanted Mifflin Co. quiltmaker used the Blockwork pattern of her people, and the acceptable color palette. The fabric is suiting, likely used for making men's coats and pants.

The quilt's current owner sees in it "plowed, not planted, fields."

19

When the Amish decide to use horsedrawn transportation, they select a pace of life that offers space for silence and reflection.

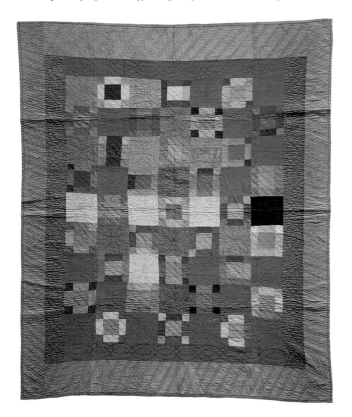

A Quilting Tradition Changes

By the mid-20th century, Amish quiltmakers were experimenting with new patterns they learned from their neighbors or discovered in newspapers.

Polyester fabrics had changed the color depths and intensities of their quilts. And women found they could finish a quilt more quickly—or make more—if they put fewer quilting stitches in each one.

The Nebraskas' quilts changed the least, although Nebraska women, too, were increasingly unable to find wool batistes and plainweave cottons. Yet they continued to reflect little influence from other groups or communities. They remained resolute followers of the established *Ordnung.*

Ironically, in their seeming disregard for aesthetics, Nebraska quiltmakers continued to create quilts with remarkable harmony. The simplicity of the quilts' structures matched their measured colors, their restrained quilting.[10] No element marched ahead of the others. While the latitude within which these women worked was tightly circumscribed, no quilt ever turned out to be exactly like another. The quiltmakers found enough room to move.

In their spareness and in their subtleties these quilts continued to hint at the secrets and the balance that hold this most conservative Amish community together.

The Bylers kept a slower pace of change than the Peacheys. Both, however, remained prepared to experiment with the possibilities brought by synthetic fibers and by greater exchange with the larger world.

Blockwork, *the Big Valley (PA), 1930, cotton feedbags, cotton, and rayon, 56 x 71, maker belonged to "White-Toppers" (Nebraska Amish), William and Connie Hayes.*

In contrast to the "wedding" quilt (page 16), this is an "everyday" quilt. There are fewer patches and they are larger; the arrangement of colors in the patchwork blocks do not serve the overall design scheme. Some of the fabrics are feedbags; one still bears the printing!

Yet the colors throughout have a nearly equivalent value, providing an overall harmony. Sober grey and tan borders surround the chaotic, pieced blocks. (Notice that the top and bottom grey border fabric has a smoother quality than the grey side borders.)

The quilting identifies this as a product of the Big Valley— double rows of diagonal stitching and cables in the borders; pinwheels in the interior plain blocks.

The quilt was made by a bishop's daughter.

Nine-Patch in Blockwork, *the Big Valley (PA), c. 1910-20, cotton, 69½ x 80, maker belonged to "Yellow-Toppers" (Byler Amish), William and Connie Hayes.*

These Nine-Patch blocks are tipped on point, giving an "at-the-ready" attitude to the quilt.

There is a basic internal order to the layout of the pieced blocks—all have pink centers; all those around the perimeter have red corner blocks, while those in the central field have pink ones. Other colors are more randomly distributed among the piecing.

The blocks of solid raspberry complement the colorfully pieced blocks. So, too, the two borders and gold binding successfully frame the active color of the central area. This quiltmaker seemed to have an intuitive sense of color value.

Cross-hatch quilting moves over the pieced blocks. More organic quilting forms fill the solid blocks and borders. The cable in the wide outer border has been expanded to five strands.

Jacob's Ladder, *the Big Valley (PA), c. 1910, cotton and wool, 69 x 80, made by Lucy A. Yoder, from the collection of Faith and Stephen Brown.*

This pattern has two basic building blocks—a Four-Patch block and a triangle.

The sense of moving diagonals and the kaleidoscope of pieced blocks comes from the careful positioning of light squares against dark.

This quiltmaker gave herself a tedious task by limiting her colors to deep blues, indigos, purples, and varying shades of black. The subtle color differences add a depth and richness to the quilt.

Cable quilting in the mauve inner border and feathery patterns in the outer border soften the whole effect.

Nine-Patch in Blockwork, *the Big Valley (PA), c. 1925-30, cotton, 74 x 83, maker belonged to Yellow-Toppers (Byler Amish), private collection.*

A plain pattern, but a playful effect. Pinks, purples, and turquoises move randomly among the uniformly pieced blocks, earning this quilt its nickname a Bubble Gum quilt.

The pieced blocks seem to stand in front of their neighboring navy blocks, demonstrating that magic can happen, despite a simple piecing design. Color choices and the positioning of blocks are equally strategic elements in creating a quilt s character.

Quilted flowers stand between the pieced blocks. Vines and bunches of grapes ring the pieced field in the outer border.

Color in Big Valley Amish Quilts, Pre-1940

Natural hues prevailed on Amish quilts made in the 1870s and '80s in the Big Valley—browns and rusts, tans of varying depths and shades, indigo blues and olive tones. These were the colors found in other communities, also, but the more muted palette persisted in Mifflin County, especially among the Nebraskas.

By the 1920s, the Bylers and the Peacheys had enlarged their color pool considerably. Brilliant pinks and oranges, yellows and purples, greens and bright blues regularly turned up in their quilt tops. What set these quilts apart was the jarring pairing of colors, often placed side by side without the steadying presence of blacks (so customary in Ohio Amish quilts) or even dark blues and browns.

Two particular colors that were often forbidden in other communities show up repeatedly on Big Valley quilts—orange and golden yellow.

The Nebraskas, as the most conservative of Amish groups, worked within the tightest boundaries, including quiltmaking. While they went beyond one-color, unpieced tops to limited forms of patchwork, they continued to use only the colors of their clothing in their quilts. That prevented their undisciplined buying of fabric or their spending too much time and energy on imaginative projects.

Nebraska Amish women wore browns and blues, plums and purples. The only black in their wardrobes were the headscarves which they used to cover their white caps. Men wore white shirts and brown pants.

Young girls' Sunday dresses could be red or green. The red and green patches that occasionally creep into a Nebraska quilt top usually came from a dress that the quiltmaker wore as a child and saved.

Sometimes orange, or another color from outside the acceptable palette, strayed into a quilt. These pieces were likely cut from fabric purchased to make dress linings or the interfacing on sleeves and hems. Because they were hidden from view, these "construction" fabrics were permitted to be of any color and were typically chosen because they happened to be on sale.[11]

One color common to many Nebraska quilts, but not worn by Nebraska women, men, or children, was a light tan. It was used frequently as a background color; apparently it was permissible to buy these goods especially for quilts.[12]

1	Kauffman, pages 54, 75.	7	Ibid, p. 24.
2	Granick, p. 95.	8	Granick, p. 95.
3	Hayes and Gleason, p. 28.	9	Ibid, p. 94.
4	Granick, p. 97.	10	Hayes and Gleason, p. 28.
5	Ibid., pp. 95, 96	11	Ibid.
6	Hayes and Gleason, p. 27.	12	Ibid.

Log Cabin, Barn-Raising Variation, *the Big Valley (PA), c. 1910-15, cotton, 64 x 69, private collection.*

These Log Cabin blocks are formed around a center square of red or olive. Five rows of black logs face five rows of alternating red and olive logs to complete each block.

Set on their flat sides the blocks' dark halves and light halves are arranged so as to make a widening set of diamonds. (Although the shades of black vary, the overall patterns is not lost.)

The triple border, with each color being the same width, underlies the strength and simplicity of the quilt's design.

Wide rows of diagonal quilting reinforce the motion of the patches' arrangement.

A Nebraska Amish farmer and his four horses prepare the soil for a new spring crop.

Cross and Four-Patch, *the Big Valley (PA), c. 1920-25, wool, 72 x 82, maker belonged to "Yellow-Toppers" (Byler Amish), private collection.*

The navy rectangles and black center squares dominate the pieced blocks in a pinwheels-at-rest attitude.

In true Big-Valley-Amish fashion, the quiltmaker surrounded the pink squares with an orange inner border. The greens and blues mediate effectively, however, so that the color combinations are pleasing rather than clashing.

The quilting on the wreaths is outstandingly fine and detailed. Pairs of stars among the feathers are a unique quilting addition.

A tiny paper note pinned to the quilt's corner tells for whom the quilt was made, likely in the hand of the quiltmaker—"For Pap's David."

Triple Irish Chain, *the Big Valley (PA), 1925, cotton, 76 x 87, private collection.*

Strategic color choices, and a well-calibrated balance between the pieced "paths" and the solid blocks, give a resolved energy to this quilt.

An abstract plant image is quilted into the large green squares. Rows of quilted sunflowers march through the outer borders.

Broken Glass, *the Big Valley (PA), 1920, cotton, 69 x 83, maker belonged to "Black-Toppers" (Peachey/Renno Amish), private collection.*

Dashes of red, orange, and black set off motion in this tightly held mass of triangles.

Most of the triangles are paired with another triangle of a contrasting color or shade. But the quiltmaker resolutely refused to establish any overall design scheme. Gentle quilting curves in the wide outer border seem to wash against the well-defined points and angles of the quilt's interior.

All the quilting is done with white thread, a departure from the more common use of black or dark colored threads used by Amish quiltmakers before 1940.

Crazy, *the Big Valley (PA), c. 1900-10, wool, 82 x 89, made for Lydia E. Kanagy, maker belonged to "Black-Toppers" (Peachey/Renno Amish), William and Connie Hayes.*

These deep rich colors show the influence of Lancaster Amish quiltmaking. But the quilting motifs are unmistakably those of the Big Valley—mulberry leaves, baskets, and hearts.

The Amish made "disciplined" Crazy quilts. The Crazy pieces were held within clear-edged blocks. The blocks were kept within one or more borders.

The brilliantly colored embroidery stitching is of a single color and pattern—pink Turkey Trot.

Nine-Patch, *the Big Valley (PA), c. 1900, wool and mohair, 70 x 82½, maker belonged to Yellow-Toppers (Byler Amish), William and Connie Hayes.*

By carefully arranging the light blue squares and dark red squares, the quiltmaker positioned the pieced blocks so as to create a rectangle within a rectangle.

Simple yet stately, this quilt includes many typical Big Valley Amish features a simple Nine-Patch design, an olive-colored fabric (which functions well as a buffer between the deep blue of the outer border, and the brighter green and purple of the inner area), and leaves and cables as quilting themes.

Triple Irish Chain Variation, *the Big Valley (PA), 1935-40, cotton, 83 x 91, maker belonged to Black-Toppers (Peachey/Renno Amish), private collection.*

    By carefully planning the layout of green and violet-blue squares within each block, and then by positioning those large blocks next to each other, the quiltmaker stopped the diagonal march of small squares across the quilt top, so customary in Irish Chain patterns. (She furthered her design scheme by placing four green rectangles around each solid green square.)

    Not only could she handle geometric complexity, the quiltmaker lavished the quilt with rows of quilted baskets in the inner border, quilted vines of mulberry leaves in the outer border, and quilted cross-hatched medallions on the unpieced green blocks.

Nebraska Amish

The Nebraskas are the most conservative group of Amish. They live in unpainted houses without carpets or curtains. Their barns are also unpainted.

During the late 1880s they came to be known as the "Nebraska Amish," after several leaders and families came from Nebraska to help a dissatisfied group within the Big Valley Amish churches. The group who eventually split were called the "Nebraskas."

The Nebraska Amish drive white-topped buggies with brown carriage boxes. Thus, their nickname—"White-Toppers."

Byler Amish

This group is often referred to as the "Byler Amish," after one of their significant leaders.

They are not as conservative as the Nebraskas, but their clothing, their painted but simply furnished homes, and their quilts, are relatively plain.

The Byler Amish drive yellow-topped buggies with black carriage bottoms. Thus, their nickname—"Yellow-Toppers."

Peachey/Renno Amish

This group was first called the "Peachey Amish," after an early leader. Later they became known as "Renno Amish," after another influential leader.

They give their homes and yards a lot of care—some wall plaques and decorative pieces are permitted; flower gardens are cultivated.

The Peachey/Renno Amish drive black-topped buggies with black carriage boxes. Thus, their nickname—"Black-Toppers."

the Big Valley (Mifflin County, PA)

The women wear long, full-skirted, two-piece dresses of browns, grays, and blues. Their head coverings are opaque and tied under the chin. They cover them with a kerchief and flat straw hat when outdoors. Men wear brown pants laced up the back, billowy white shirts, and straw hats with wide brims.

Quilt Characteristics

Nebraska quilters were restricted by the church in both the patterns and the colors they may use. Basic piecing patterns are Nine-Patch, Four-Patch, and Blockwork. Available colors are browns, blues, plums, purples, tans. Quilting motifs are primarily straight rows, (often on the diagonal), chains, and fans.

The women wear dresses with full skirts, capes, and aprons, in dark colors. Their head coverings are white; their bonnets, worn outdoors, are of brown fabric. Men support their pants with a single suspender, worn diagonally over the right shoulder, and often wear blue chambray shirts.

Quilt Characteristics

The Bylers often chose Blockwork and Four- and Nine-Patch designs, although they did more intricate piecing, such as Irish Chain, Jacob's Ladder, and Tumbling Blocks patterns.

Their color palette was extensive—from bright pinks and oranges to blacks and sea greens.

They often chose to quilt a vine of blackberry leaves or chains, fans, or hearts through the borders.

The women wear dark dresses with full skirts, capes, and aprons. Their head coverings are white; their black bonnets have a high crown and a bow in the back. Men's shirts have buttons; pants are held up by a single suspender, crossing diagonally over the right shoulder.

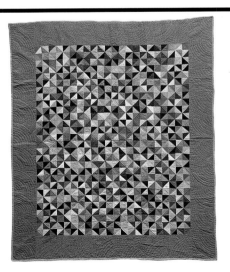

Quilt Characteristics

Quilts made by members of the Peachey/Renno group show greater influence from other Amish communities than those made by the Nebraskas, or even the Bylers.

Quiltmakers seem to have chosen patterns free of cautions by the church. They, too, do Blockwork, but also Log Cabins, Shoofly, and Crazies, often in brilliant, but plain, colors. Golden yellow, bright blues, purples, and vibrant greens stand side by side. Favorite quilting themes are Sprucie Hearts, pinwheels, baskets, tulips, and hearts within hearts.

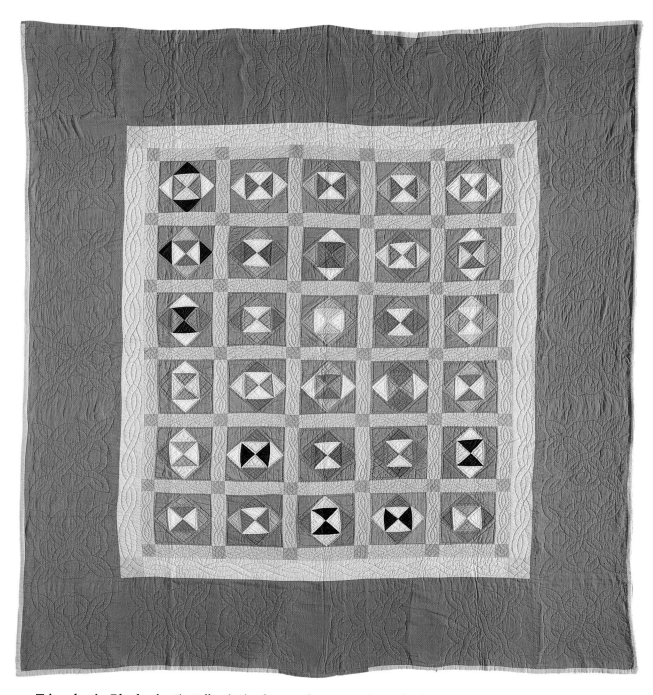

Triangles in Block, *the Big Valley (PA), photograph courtesy of David Wheatcroft.*

Although each block is composed of 12 triangles and each is constructed by the same pattern, some blocks appear to have a decidedly horizontal orientation, while others appear to be vertical. In fact, the attitude of each block results from the varying color values of the facing triangles within it.

In addition, the placement of the yellow triangles within each block affects whether that block appears to lie horizontally or vertically. (Only one block has no yellow triangles. On the bottom row, the center block substitutes peach triangles for yellow.)

The delicately colored sashing and corner blocks, as well as the shades of blue in the borders, allow each pieced block to be seen individually.

The unusually wide outer border exhibits quilting resembling intertwining vegetation.

The pieced binding is typical of many Big Valley quilts.

Album/Bars, *the Big Valley (PA), "March 1943" embroidered on back, cotton, 67 x 81, maker belonged to "Black-Toppers" (Peachey/Renno Amish), private collection.*

A piecing showcase—42 different patterns—on one side of this reversible quilt; a simple Bars on the other.
If unexpected visitors came who may not have approved of the flair demonstrated in all the piecing, the quiltmaker sent her children upstairs to flip the quilt over to the Bars side, thereby showing a humbler, Ordnung-approved approach!

Nine-Patch on Point, *the Big Valley (PA), 1895, wool and cotton, 64 x 77, maker belonged to "White-Toppers" (Nebraska Amish), private collection.*

The strong colors of the solid blocks, matched by the steady rhythm of the pieced blocks, produce vertical columns that seem to zigzag from top to bottom.

The muted, home-dyed colors bring a restraint to the quilt, but the sometimes unexpected appearance of purple and light blue, and the surprising substitution of colors, add energy and freedom.

The quilting on the interior field is well planned—a flat tulip in the center row of solid blocks, grapes in the next rows of solid blocks moving out from the center, and lamb's tongue in the triangles along the sides, top, and bottom of the interior section.

Roman Coin Variation Crib, *the Big Valley (PA),*
c. 1920-25, cotton, 38½ x 47, private collection.

A mix of planning and spontaneity! Most blocks have five strips; some have six. The pieced squares are all nearly the same size, although their strips vary in width. The pieced squares have been arranged so that in some, their strips angle to the right; in others, they angle to the left. The sequence of colors changes from block to block. Perhaps this was a learning quilt for the baby's older sister.

Double rows of straight stitching through the pieced blocks, and double hearts within the solid blocks, are traditional Mifflin County quilting practices.

Variable Star Variation Crib, *the Big Valley (PA),*
1920, cotton, 42 x 57, private collection.

This lovely delicate quilt seems to carry affection for a child, as well as for quiltmaking.

Consistently pieced triangles and squares are used, instead of the rectangular pieces that typically surround blockwork in Mifflin County quilts.

The quiltmaker brought out a full repertoire of quilting motifs. The maple leaves in the inner grey border are unusually well executed.

Sunshine and Shadow, *the Big Valley (PA), c. 1930-35, cotton, 72 x 78, maker belonged to "Yellow-Toppers" (Byler Amish), private collection.*

Located between the two largest Amish communities in the world (Holmes County, Ohio, and Lancaster County, Pennsylvania), the Amish of the Big Valley show influence from both areas in their quilts.

The Sunshine and Shadow pattern is a favorite Lancaster design. The use of black to create high contrast with surrounding colors is an Ohio practice.

The pairing of pink and orange, and orange and purple, is typical of Big Valley quilters, who often used jarring color combinations.

The mulberry-leaf motif quilted into the outer border is a distinctive Big Valley design.

The black inner border runs only along the sides, displaying another Big Valley characteristic—not insisting that borders be uniform the whole way around.

Four in Blockwork on Point, *the Big Valley (PA), 1910, cotton, 81 x 91, maker belonged to "Black-Toppers" (Peachey/Renno Amish), private collection.*

This orderly quilt is quintessentially Big Valley Amish—Four-Patch blocks held within blockwork; a strong grid (provided by the light blue and beige squares running in vertical rows; the brown squares running horizontally); the mulberry-leaf quilting motif in the top and bottom outer borders.

But it has a few atypical features. The large unpieced blocks in the inner field are made of a print fabric. The quilt is remarkably symmetrical and routine with a minimum of variations. (A few of the small light blocks in a patch lying in the second row from the top, the second patch in from the right, appear to be light mauve rather than blue.)

Green Market, New York

The first day of false spring, I hit the street,
buoyant, my coat open. I could keep walking
and leave that job without cleaning my desk.
At Union Square the country people slouch
by crates of last fall's potatoes.
An Amish lady tends her table of pies.
I ask where her farm is. "Upstate," she says,
"but we moved from P.A. where the land is better,
and the growing season's longer by a month."
I ask where in P.A. "Towns you wouldn't know,
around Mifflinburg, around Belleville."
And I tell her I was born there.
"Now who would your grandparents be?"
"Thomas and Vesta Peachey."
"Well, I was a Peachey," she says,
and she grins like she sees the whole farm
on my face. "What a place your folks had,
down Locust Grove. Do you know my father,
the harness shop on the Front Mountain Road?"
I do. And then we can't think of what to say,
that Valley so far from the traffic on Broadway.
I choose a pie while she eyes my short hair
then looks square on my face. She knows
I know better than to pay six dollars for this.
"Do you live in the city?" she asks. "Do you like it?"
I say no. And that was no lie, Emma Peachey.
I don't like New York, but sometimes these streets
hold me as hard as we're held by rich earth.
I have not forgotten that Bible verse:
Whoever puts his hand to the plow and looks back
is not fit for the kingdom of God.

—Julia Kasdorf

Julia Spicher Kasdorf was born into the Mennonite and Amish community of Mifflin County, Pennsylvania, in 1962. She was raised in Irwin, Pennsylvania, near Pittsburgh, and attended Goshen (IN) College and New York University, where she received her undergraduate and graduate degrees. Her poems have appeared in the New Yorker *and many other publications. "Green Market, New York" was first published in* Festival Quarterly, *Fall 1989.*

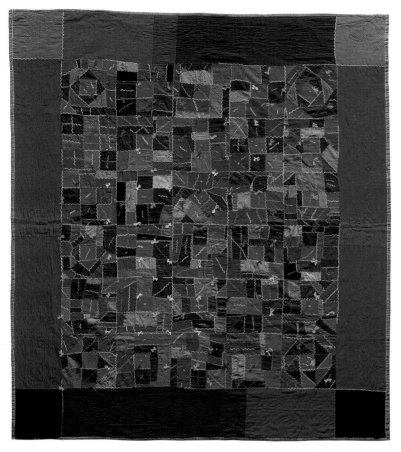

Crazy, *the Big Valley (PA), c. 1925-30, cotton, 76 x 89, private collection.*

Thirty blocks, each full of irregular but richly colored patches, each an exercise in a variety of brilliantly bright embroidery stitches. (Yarn knots spaced across the interior of the quilt do the work of holding the batting in place.)

An austere border with corner blocks surrounds the more playful patches. Quilted fern leaves spill from color to color.

Sunshine and Shadow Diagonal, *the Big Valley (PA), c. 1920-25, wool, 76 x 85, maker belonged to "Yellow-Toppers" (Byler Amish), private collection.*

Simple in its piecing but dramatic in its color arrangement, this quilt shows that many shades of red can work pleasingly together. Key to the harmony are strategically placed rows of blues and greens.

The sea-green inner border keeps the overall effect from becoming heavy.

Straight lines running on an angle continue in the quilting. Only the inner border offers a curvilinear strand of quilting.

Two Amish sisters at home—with their quilt and with each other.

(on next page)

Flower Garden, *the Shenandoah Valley (VA), c. 1942, cotton, 75 x 90, made by Flora May (Flossie) Grove Showalter (a member of Trissels Mennonite Church) for her daughter Kathryn Showalter Shank at the time of her marriage, private collection.*

The patches in this Flower Garden are a geometric showcase. Each yellow center has six sides and is surrounded by six blue, six-sided pieces. Each ring, as it moves outward from the center, numbers pieces that are multiples of six: the print fabric rings have 12 pieces, the cream rings have 18, the teal rings 24.

Modest in its tone, yet precisely rendered, this is a typical Mennonite quilt. The print fabrics may have come from worn-out dresses, which were paired with plain fabrics, likely bought for this use—a common practice of frugal Mennonites.

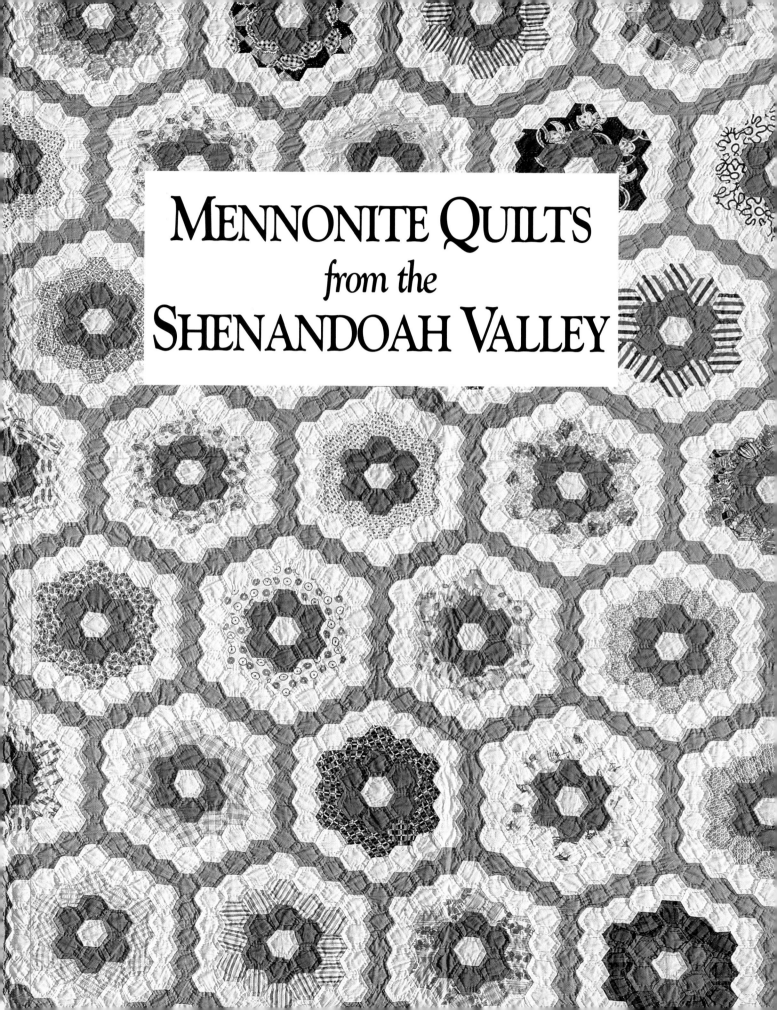

MENNONITE QUILTS
from the
SHENANDOAH VALLEY

The Mennonites of Virginia's Shenandoah Valley

The Shenandoah Valley holds its breathless beauty yet today. In the beginnings of the 18th century, this lovely vein of a valley was alluring pioneer territory for Mennonites—both enterprising ones, as well as those looking for a hopeful fresh start.

The earliest records tell of German-speaking settlers moving in from Pennsylvania about 1727. Some came

Flower Baskets, *the Shenandoah Valley (VA), pieced c. 1930-40, quilted c. 1950, cotton, 84 x 90, pieced by Lydia Hess Rohrer (a member of Bank Mennonite Church), quilted by Lydia's daughter Mabel Rohrer Cline and her daughter Ruth Cline Shank, the current owner with her husband, Joseph.*

This orderly quilt involves a set of geometric shapes for each patch—a square, rectangles, diamonds, and triangles of various sizes.

The patches are identical, except for the lower pairs of petals that rest on the baskets' top edges. The pair of petals always matches each other, but they change from patch to patch.

The green and yellow solid fabrics provide an effective platform for the quilting so that the quilted unpieced squares (set on point) have as much interest as the pieced patches.

because they believed that the best land in eastern Pennsylvania (where many of their compatriots had made a new home) had already been claimed. Others may have been edgy about volatile relationships with native Americans in parts of Pennsylvania. Still others came hoping for favorable economic conditions; William Penn's sons had tightened up land policies, collecting rents and taxes more regularly than had been done before.

In the early to mid-18th century, the 150-mile-long stretch of Valley was certainly less developed than the eastern areas of Virginia. Not daunted by the mountains and their thick forests and streams, Mennonite families were drawn to the rolling Valley hills and their possibilities for cultivation. Governor Gooch, who in the 1730s and '40s required all who lived in the eastern part of the state to belong to the Church of England, relaxed his religious rules for settlers west of the Blue Ridge Mountains. If they were willing to tame the frontier and fend off the native Americans, they could be rewarded with religious liberties, he seemed to reason. Mennonites and Quakers were among those who rose to the opportunity.

By 1773 there were Shanks, Brennemans, Burkholders, Kauffmans, Coffmans, Wengers, and Beerys, from Edom north to Broadway. More families with traditional Mennonite names were farming west of Broadway—Brunks, Showalters, Branners, Drivers, Rohrers, and Geils.

Sample family inventories from 1746 and 1749 list livestock, horses, and hogs, many farm implements, some household furniture and clothing, ironware, and bees. One includes "two old blankets"; another mentions "bed clothes." These same two list old books and Bibles; one singles out a "great Martyrs Book" and "ten small books called Golden Apples." There are no references to quilts.

The Mennonite Community Takes Shape

Not only were these Mennonite households stabilizing their economic standing, they were establishing their faith community as well. In the beginning, families met for worship in homes, perhaps for economic reasons, perhaps for political reasons. They were not financially prepared to erect a church building. Sometimes nicknamed "German Quakers," they may have also been discouraged from meeting for worship in a commonwealth

Old Order Mennonites of Virginia strengthen their sense of community by visiting.

that officially frowned on religious assemblies that were not part of the Church of England.

Several other religious groups and movements chipped away at the Mennonites who were working to put their religious ballast in place. The "Great Awakening" sent missionaries into the Valley, stirring hope in certain subdued congregations, causing havoc in others. The more expressive Baptists drew some Mennonites away. Other Mennonites found the religious upheaval a time to reflect on issues that frequently distinguished them from other religious peoples—matters such as refusing to participate in slavery, war, and swearing oaths. The neighboring Dunkers stimulated their thinking about appropriate baptism and communion practices.

This was not a relaxing time for Virginia Mennonites. Land ownership snafus threatened several settlements. They discovered double and even triple claims to some of their original land grants, throwing households into considerable uncertainty. Did they have legal title to their land? Would they have to pay for their land again?

Some Mennonites left the disputed areas and moved further south, spreading Shanks, Coffmans, Blossers, Brubakers, Goods, Bowmans, Funks, Longs, Stauffers, and Groves into the lower section of the Valley.

Virginia was not free of tensions with native Americans. The French and Indian War aggravated relationships, and here and there white settlers died, probably several Mennonites among them. Some who felt uneasy and vulnerable returned to Pennsylvania in the 1750s and '60s, seeking the safety of a more established community.

Yet by the 1820s, enough of a group had taken root throughout the reach of the Valley that Mennonite

Queen Anne Medallion, *the Shenandoah Valley (VA), c. late 1920s, cotton sateen, 78 x 80, made by Lydia Frances Lahman Shank (August 8, 1875-August 20, 1959) for her daughter Fannie Bell Shank Heatwole, mother of the current owner, John and his wife, Mary Ann, Heatwole.*

Lydia Frances Lahman Shank enjoyed quilting—straight lines, curves, and tiny circles. She made a series of these whole-cloth quilts, perhaps as many as eight, in a variety of pastel colors, among them lavender, yellow, and peach.

This quilt is designed to be reversible. Its other side is cream-colored.

47

Mennonite sewing circles and women's groups in the Valley make quilts today to sell at the annual Augusta County Mennonite Relief Auction. Crowds flock to the Sale, eager to bid on and buy quilts that are known for their remarkable workmanship.

church buildings began to appear. Nearly 100 years after their arrival, Mennonites were finding it difficult to accommodate a congregation in their homes for worship. Perhaps they began building partly to stem the pull that the Baptists and United Brethren (both of whom met in churches) were having on Mennonite membership. Fear of persecution was nearly forgotten; instead, attention had moved to maintaining their own fellowships.

Virginia Mennonites Organize Officially

No longer struggling simply to survive, Virginia Mennonites of the 1820s and '30s began to disengage from

Suns and Stars, *the Shenandoah Valley (VA), pieced 1931-37, quilted in the mid-1960s, cotton, 68½ x 89, Mary Deputy Brubaker.*

Mary Deputy Brubaker, now in her mid-80s, spends much of her time quilting. It has been a satisfying tie to her past and tradition, even when she entered new territory (she helped to establish the nursing education department in the early 1960s at Eastern Mennonite University in Harrisonburg, Virginia).

This quilt commemorates significant events in her personal history. The green fabric is from the dress she wore when she was baptized; the yellow comes from the dress she wore the day she entered nurse's training; the lavender is from the dress she had on the day she suffered such a severe toothache she had to have the tooth extracted.

A ring of lavender hexagons surrounds the center sun; lavender points transform yellow hexagons into stars (as do the stars quilted within those yellow blocks).

the Lancaster (PA) Conference, which had given a degree of leadership to the early congregations in the Valley. The Shenandoah Mennonites were ready to form their own leadership structure. In 1835 they called a conference for fellowship, but also to work at difficult matters, so as not to lose a basic unity.

They discussed major issues—singing schools (permitted), slavery (not permitted), life insurance (were they failing to trust God and their co-members if they carried it?), lawsuits (didn't they employ inappropriate use of force?), "faithful" dress patterns, the pluses and minuses of Sunday schools and revival meetings, who may participate in communion, and what is the meaning of ordination. Other difficult topics were whether to switch from German to English in worship services (at the risk of losing their historical roots and contemporary distinctiveness, while increasing the influence of other related, but different, Christian groups) and what worship styles and forms of music were fitting for Mennonites.

Easy Exchange with Neighbors

Stretched over the length of the Shenandoah Valley, clusters of Mennonites took on different flavors and character. They reflected their neighbors, the original communities from which they had come, and the concerns and emphases of their leaders.

The campus of Eastern Mennonite University lies near the Massanutten Peak in Harrisonburg, Virginia. The University receives strong support from Virginia Conference Mennonites.

Had they been more concentrated geographically, they may have been a more insular group. But their scatteredness likely led to their greater exchange with neighbors. They shared the Valley with the English and Scots-Irish. For the Mennonites who were dwarfed in numbers, the English language became almost a necessity. When the Bank Church was built in 1860, Preacher David Rhodes "opened" the church by preaching in English. Contrary to the practice elsewhere, the congregation had built no schoolhouse nearby, seeming to indicate that they were no longer formally teaching German to their children.

Not all Virginia Mennonites had been persuaded to relinquish German, however. In the 1820s, as German began to give way to English and church buildings replaced worshipping in homes, a staunch group resisted the movement. They were not an isolated fragment, but were represented in the Northern, Middle, and Lower Districts of Virginia Conference. They were harbingers of a later, more decisive, divide.

There were tensions within the increasingly established Virginia churches; there was growing unease with slavery practiced on neighboring farms to the Mennonites; there was the constant effort to make the orchards, the field crops, and the cattle profitable.

A Church Division Occurs

Although the Mennonites opposed slavery and participating in the military, the Civil War left many marks on them (see page 56).

In the years following the War, and as recovery from it began to require less energy, the church turned its focus to its ongoing life. Interest in Sunday schools resurfaced in many places, although not everywhere. In fact, the formation of Sunday schools became a major grievance for a group who had been increasingly concerned about the general direction of the Virginia Mennonite Conference. This group believed that the Conference leaders, and many of their constituency, were emphasizing the wrong issues— including mission activity and the way in which leaders were chosen.

During 1901-02, the two groups divided into what came to be known as the Old Order Mennonites and Virginia Mennonite Conference. It had been a long and laborious disturbance with many efforts made to find common ground, agreed-upon authority, and reconciliation.

This was not the last division to occur among Mennonites within the Valley. In 1971 the Southeastern Mennonite Conference was formed, the result of a withdrawal of a series of congregations from Virginia Conference.

Farmer s Delight, *the Shenandoah Valley (VA), 1878, cotton, 68 x 83¹/₂, made by Mary Virginia Rhodes Brenneman (1848-1925, and a member of the Old Order Mennonites), great-aunt of the current owner, Fred and his wife, Alma H., Wenger.*

A piecing and quilting wonder! Twelve-petaled flowers float in the center of each ring. Every flower has six pink petals; half of the flowers have six green petals; half have six yellow petals.

The yellow fabric must have run a bit short; substitute fabrics were used in two of the flowers. And the flower in the bottom left corner is a well-disguised mis-match its petals are larger, and a dark red fabric replaces the pink.

The double ring surrounding the flowers are each made up of 50-75 triangles (the numbers fluctuate from ring to ring). The Flying Geese side borders are also streams of triangles.

Mary Virginia Rhodes Brenneman must have enjoyed quilting as much as piecing. The clam shell design is created with minute and even stitching, validating Virginia Mennonite quiltmakers claim of being finer quilters than the Lancaster Amish !

Mary Virginia (known as Aunt Polly) quilted her initials and the date of the quilt into the small medallion just above the center. MVB and 1878 lie on their sides, nearly obscured, perhaps indicating Aunt Polly s mix of pride and humility.

Mennonite Quilts from the Shenandoah Valley, Pre-1940

As people migrate, so do quilt patterns. When the Mennonites moved into the Shenandoah Valley from southeastern and southcentral Pennsylvania, they brought their favorite quilt designs with them.

As they had time and money, they turned those visual memories and wrinkly paper patterns into quilts. And as they became more established, they shared their know-how with their neighbors, and learned from them in turn.

The Mennonites who settled between Virginia s Appalachian and Blue Ridge mountains created a sprinkling of little strongholds up and down the Valley. But those communities of like faith and practice had porous boundaries. The Mennonites were an identifiable people, yet they had friendly exchange with those they lived among.

It seems likely that some of the English and Scots-Irish who found their way from eastern Virginia over the mountains into this Valley brought their quilting traditions also. Whole-cloth quilts, embellished with quilted medallions, and strippy patterns, both commonly made in the British Isles, appeared in Virginia. Some Mennonites eventually tried these styles, willing to broaden their repertoire beyond the family of patterns they brought from their grandmothers and home areas.

Shenandoah Valley Quilt Patterns

Some Shenandoah Valley Mennonites made whole-cloth quilts of pastel, plain-colored fabrics and covered them with swirls of quilting and crosshatching. Many more, however, chose their piecing designs from the stock of folk art images that were common in the Mid-Atlantic area throughout the 19th century. These abstracted, highly pieced designs included stars, leaves, flowers, and feathers. Others were repeating geometric patterns, made of tiny patches of fabric placed together to create straight rows or diagonal action.

These women drew upon a set of designs that may have first emerged in central Europe, and then traveled with German-speaking immigrants to eastern Pennsylvania, taking on new features as they moved to new communities. These usually orderly, balanced designs seemed to hold appeal for these tidy, restrained women. In fact, the quiltmakers planned their quilts with great care; most of the bedcovers show fastidious attention to exact repetition of pattern and the careful positioning of colors.

Shenandoah Valley Mennonites were not restricted by their church to designated quilt patterns and colors. But their own ethnic origins and migration histories provided them with a set of designs and a sense of harmony and discipline that they found appealing and that is displayed on most of their pre-1940 quilts.

The quilts from this community frequently bear the deeply rich, brilliant colors of those made by Mennonites

Flower Baskets, *the Shenandoah Valley (VA), c. 1900, cotton, 81 1/2 x 88, made by Hannah and Mary Elizabeth (Molly) Brenneman (members of the Mt. Carmel Church at Fulks Run), great-aunts of the current owner.*

The Brenneman sisters were single and lived together, working cooperatively at their quiltmaking.

The individual patches in their Flower Baskets quilt take on particular character because of the way in which some of the contrasting triangles were assembled to form the petals. When the dark and light triangles were flip-flopped, the resulting petals look somewhat hapless, as though victims of a strong wind.

Because of the way the Basket blocks were sewn together with the solid red squares, the quilt appears to be wider than it is long.

51

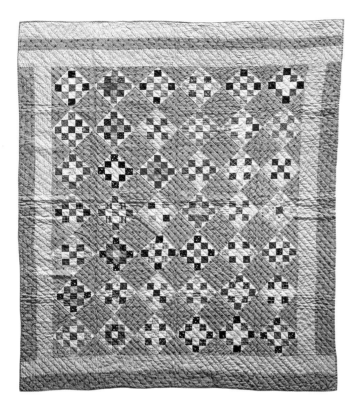

Blockwork, *the Shenandoah Valley (VA), c. 1910, cotton, 67 x 80½, made by Lillie Hess Trissel (a member of Weavers Mennonite Church) and mother of the current owner, Fern C. Trissel.*

Thirteen square blocks in a mixture of light and dark fabrics, along with 12 light-colored triangles, made up the 42 patches in this quilt. Each patch appears to have been "composed."

The unpieced blocks add a tone of neutrality to the visual activity of the pieced patches.

The borders also indicate that the quilt was carefully planned, despite its unobtrusive colors and simplicity of pattern.

Drunkard's Path, *the Shenandoah Valley (VA), c. 1950, cotton, 77 x 93, made by Anna Showalter Shank (a member of the Old Order Mennonite Church) for her son Kenneth and his wife, Carolyn, Shank.*

Anna Showalter Shank made this quilt for her son Kenneth. In fact, she made Drunkard's Path quilts for each of her three sons, each one a different color. Joseph's is green and white; John Robert's is dark red and white. (Her three daughters received quilts of different patterns.)

Anna learned the love of quiltmaking from her mother, Wilda Brunk Showalter, who made a quilt for each of her grandchildren, firmly establishing the tradition of making quilts to pass on within the family.

A member of the Old Order Mennonites, Wilda's daughter Anna was not restricted to working only with dark colors. Nor was there pressure from the church community to skimp on the amount or fineness of quilting.

in Pennsylvania's Lancaster and Adams counties. Others use pastels, demonstrating the influence of neighbors on these women.

Many of these quilts are constructed with multiple borders and sashing—typical Lancaster characteristics.

Many show the effect of Lancaster traditions on their quilting motifs. Crosshatching and borders full of quilted vines and feathers are quite customary. But Virginia quilters have their own pride. "We do much finer quilting than they do in Lancaster," many current Shenandoah Valley Mennonite quilters assert when asked what distinguishes their quilts. "We *cover* them with quilting, and our stitches are *much* tinier! In Lancaster, they try to get a quilt out by 2 in the afternoon [at a quilting bee]. They like to talk about how often they 'roll' [a reference to the practice of rolling up a quilt that is stretched on a frame, as sections of it are fully quilted by the women seated around the frame].

"Well, around here, we may roll only a couple of times in a day. We're putting in so many stitches, it just takes longer!"

So while it is very difficult to pinpoint distinctive Shenandoah Valley Mennonite quilt patterns, it is possible to trace the piecing and quilting designs that these quiltmakers selected to pattern "families" and people migrations. But what is almost uniformly true of pre-1940 Mennonite quilts, especially those made in the Shenandoah Valley, are their precise piecing, their symmetry and balance, their geometric images, their fine, full quilting.

Irish Chain, *the Shenandoah Valley (VA), c. 1880, cotton, 75 x 85, pieced by Anna Showalter Trissel (d. 1881) for her youngest son, David; quilted by Anna's daughter Barbara Trissel Blosser, currently owned by Iva M. Trissel.*

This stately quilt demonstrates the strength of well-matched and carefully balanced primary colors.
Rather than receding, the large fields of white hold their own next to the deep red and blue squares, because of their lavishly detailed quilting.
The triple border, with each color represented and with each strip the approximate width of the pieced squares, adds a well-proportioned frame.

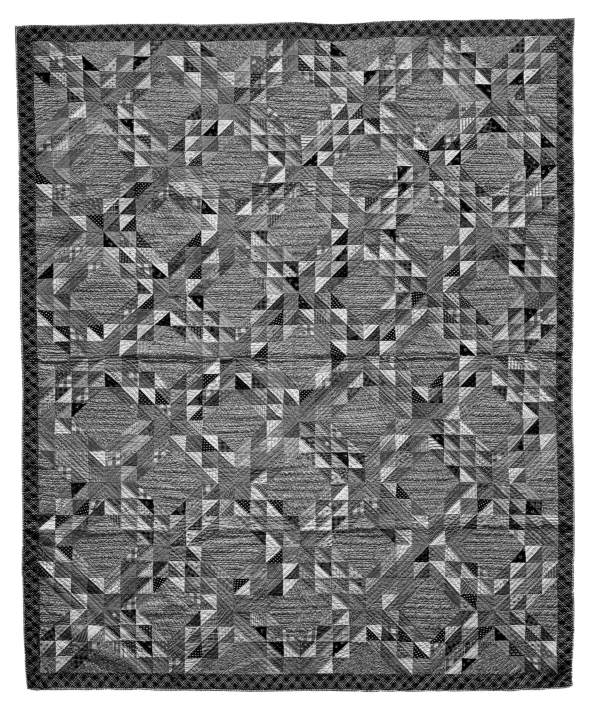

Ocean Waves, *the Shenandoah Valley (VA), c. 1885, cotton, 68 x 85, made by Fannie Showalter (1867-1888 and a member of Trissels Mennonite Church) and aunt of the current owner, Howard and his wife, Irene, Showalter.*

Mennonite quiltmakers in most communities have not been restricted to plain fabrics. Instead, they have regularly used prints and plaids, checks and stripes. That may be freeing, but it also requires considerable management. Maintaining an overall design while using highly patterned pieces of fabric demands both daring and care.

Even the unpieced blocks in this Ocean Waves quilt are full of figures. Yet they provide an almost neutral effect to the actively-patterned triangles that seem to whiz by.

Notice that wherever the diagonal rows of triangles crisscross, a square of eight triangles is formed, momentarily quieting the motion. In each of those 32 squares over the face of the quilt, red is a recurring color.

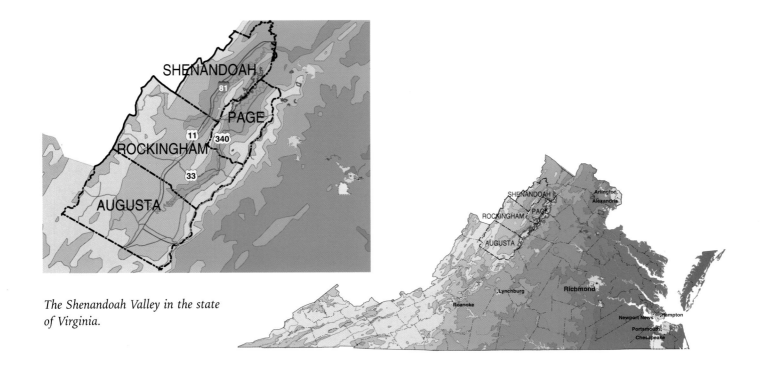

The Shenandoah Valley in the state of Virginia.

Virginia Mennonites in the Civil War

The Civil War brought new pressures to all the Mennonites of the Shenandoah Valley. They were aligned by geography with the Confederacy, despite their abhorrence of slavery and war, and their disinterest in political activity. For a time, they were able to maintain their status as conscientious objectors by paying a fee rather than attending drills. But as the war effort intensified, Mennonite men took a variety of routes to avoid joining the military—some hid, some fled, others hired substitutes to take their places, some were forced into active duty (although some of those refused to shoot).

At times they were granted exemption, provided they paid substantial fees, only to have those deals withdrawn or compromised when the Confederacy grew increasingly threatened. At the least, Mennonite farm families had their crops and horses scavenged by the southern armies, who learned that the fertile farmlands of the Valley were a prime place to refuel.

In fact, it was the Valley's store of food for both men and animals that made it the target of Union General Sheridan. He systematically destroyed its standing and stored crops, its cattle, barns, and mills, in an effort to deprive Confederate armies of their food supplies. That successful destruction spurred dozens of Mennonite households, as well as many young men in their mid-teens, to leave the Valley for the North, at least temporarily.

Artist J. E. Taylor drew this scene of about 100 Mennonites and Dunkers receiving passes to go to the North. The encampment was in the foothills of Massanutten Peak. Photograph courtesy of Samuel Horst and Western Reserve Historical Society.

Those that stayed turned to rebuilding.

Reestablishing farms was a slow process. There was too little labor and too little working equipment; there was devalued Confederate money and a too-distant Industrial Revolution to revitalize these rural communities quickly.

Some Mennonites from the North were drawn to the Shenandoah Valley for its low, post-War land prices. And so the interchange between Pennsylvania and Virginia Mennonites continued, communities crisscrossing in these years of war-time trauma.

Fencerow, *the Shenandoah Valley (VA), c. 1950, cotton, 81½ x 94, made by Wilda G. Showalter (a member of the Old Order Mennonites) and grandmother of the current owner, Kenneth and his wife, Carolyn, Shank.*

Although she used numerous fabrics to make the dozens of triangles needed for her fencerow patches, Wilda left no doubt about the overall design of her quilt top.

In fact, she may have had a rather quiet end result had she not framed it with the teal inner border. That color choice electrifies the many tones and shades in the pieced paths.

Wilda pieced this quilt by hand, seeing to it manually that point met point and that the sides were cleanly straight.

This is one of 24 quilts she made for her grandchildren. She was the mother of 12 children, four of whom died within two days of their births. Wilda G. Showalter, born in 1889, lived to be 101 years old.

Fan, *the Shenandoah Valley (VA), piecing c. 1930; quilting c. 1970, cotton, 82 x 96½, pieced by Fannie Susan Heatwole Deputy, quilted by four generations of Fannie's descendants, currently owned by Mary Deputy Brubaker.*

The building blocks of this Fan are the same as the more traditional arrangements of this pattern. The Fan center (one-fourth of a circle) is edged by a series of narrow spokes which together appear to nestle into one corner of a square block.

Grandma Fannie achieved the look of 12 floral wreaths by the way in which she positioned 16 square blocks to form each wreath. Her daughters and nieces (of several generations) reinforced her design scheme by quilting unifying floral motifs wherever the large cream sections of four blocks come together.

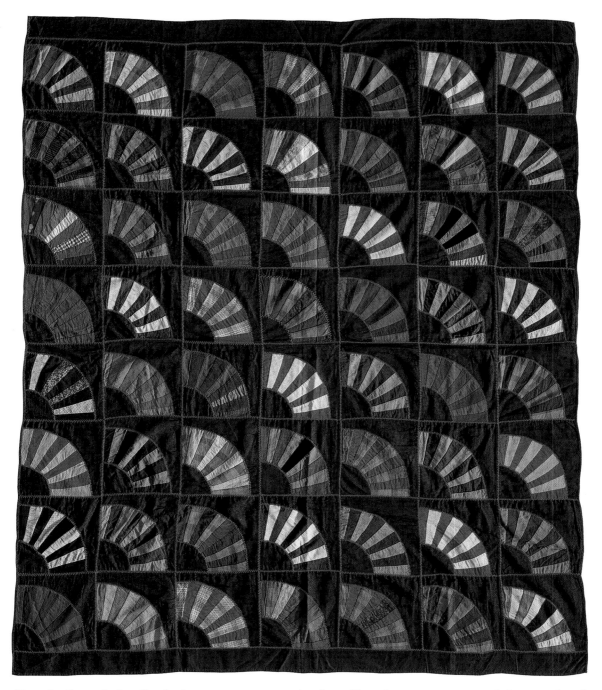

Fan, *the Shenandoah Valley (VA), c. 1900, cotton, wool, velvet, silk, and sateen, 63 x 77, made by Hannah and Mary Elizabeth (Molly) Brenneman, (members of the Mt. Carmel Church at Fulks Run), great-aunts of the current owner.*

The format is simple and well defined (and more common than the arrangement on the facing page): the background of each block is black; the Fan "spokes" alternate between dark and light pieces; red turkey trot embroidery stitching outlines each block and each Fan.

The same fabrics reappear over the face of the quilt, yet it seems that quiltmakers Hannah and Molly Brenneman intended to make each block different from every other block in the combination of fabrics they used.

Notice the wide variety of fabrics—cotton, wools, velvet, silk, and sateen.

The quilt has a top and bottom border, but no side borders.

Hens and "PeePees" *(baby chicks), the Shenandoah Valley (VA), 1938, cotton, 77 x 85, pieced by Emma Martin Rhodes (a member of the Old Order Mennonites), quilted by Mary Rohrer, currently owned by Grace, Oliver, and Harry Burkholder.*

Grace Burkholder, for whom this quilt was made, believes that her grandmother bought several bolts of these fabrics expressly to make quilts for her grandchildren. Several quilts of these colors, but of different patterns, are owned by her descendants. Despite the conservative and sober nature of the church to which Emma Martin Rhodes belonged, she was free to choose garish colors for her quilts!

The quilt pattern likely inspired its farm-fresh name—tiny chicks cluster close to the warmth of their mother hen, just as the yellow and lavender triangles hover around the red squares, and the lavender and yellow triangles around the yellow squares.

The red squares, tipped on point, draw the eye, but the yellow and lavender squares and triangles function as full partners.

Wishing Ring, *the Shenandoah Valley (VA), c. 1920, cotton, 70¹/₂ x 84, made by Emma Martin Rhodes (a member of the Old Order Mennonites), currently owned by Grace, Oliver, and Harry Burkholder.*

A clean, crisp pattern, executed in colors of compatible intensity. The flying geese borders on three sides add some movement to an otherwise static quilt.

The top border is formed by pairs of teal and white triangles placed on both sides of a long strip of teal fabric. But here the triangles are handled differently than on the other three borders. The quiltmaker chose a sort of zig-zag, sizzle action, in contrast to the single motion present on the other three borders.

The quilting is plentiful a single vine with occasional leaves threads through the teal border strips; simple flowers soften the 12 squares in the central field; straight lines crisscross the main body of the quilt.

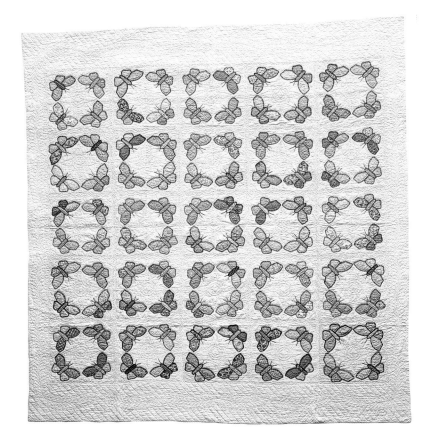

Butterfly Applique Quilt, *the Shenandoah Valley (VA), begun c. 1938, completed c. 1942, cotton, 89 x 96, appliqued and assembled by Elizabeth Heatwole Grove (a member of Weavers Mennonite Church and mother of the current owner), quilted by Becky Heatwole, currently owned by Richard and Virginia Grove Weaver.*

Rather than hiding her applique stitches, Elizabeth made them a feature of these 100 butterflies. Held motionless, the butterflies are positioned to create a field of wreath-like images, a favorite piecing and quilting motif.

Becky Heatwole, considered one of the best quilters in the area at the time, continued the circular theme by quilting large centers for the flowers within each butterfly circle, and at the corners whenever two or more blocks meet.

Stars, *the Shenandoah Valley, c. 1925-30, cotton, 69½ x 79½, made by Pearl Blosser Suter, grandmother of the current owner, Harriet Harman Steiner.*

In this carefully executed quilt, none of the pieced Stars is alike, although they are all studiously consistent. Each six-pointed inner Star is surrounded by a ring of contrasting pieces. The outer six points of each Star are a gentle pink, matching the pink inner and outer borders around the quilt s sides and bottom. (The outer pink border was not added to the top).

This quilt was made by Pearl Blosser Suter, grandmother of the current owner. Suter is a Shenandoah Valley Mennonite name, often associated with fine craftsmanship. Daniel Suter was a well-known cabinetmaker. He had two children who are remembered for their strong workmanship Emanuel, the potter, and Margaret, a weaver and seamstress.

A love of artistry extended further into the family. This quilt s maker was married to J. Early Suter, the son of Emanuel Suter s son John.

Dresden Plate, *the Shenandoah Valley (VA), 1938, cotton, 72, x 81, pieced by Minnie Atchison (great-aunt of current owner), quilted by Anna May Weaver Driver and Gladys Driver (mother and sister of current owner; both Minnie and Anna May were members of Weavers Mennonite Church), currently owned by Brownie M. Driver.*

Wheels of pieced color and full quilting alternate over the face of this quilt. The quilted circles are so precisely realized that they seem to be mirror imprints of the pieced plates.

Although the piecer and the quilters spanned three generations, each seems to have had a full grasp of a quilt s essence, and the techniques needed to realize it.

The love of pastels, the careful design, the lush quilting all are hallmarks of Mennonite quiltmaking of this period.

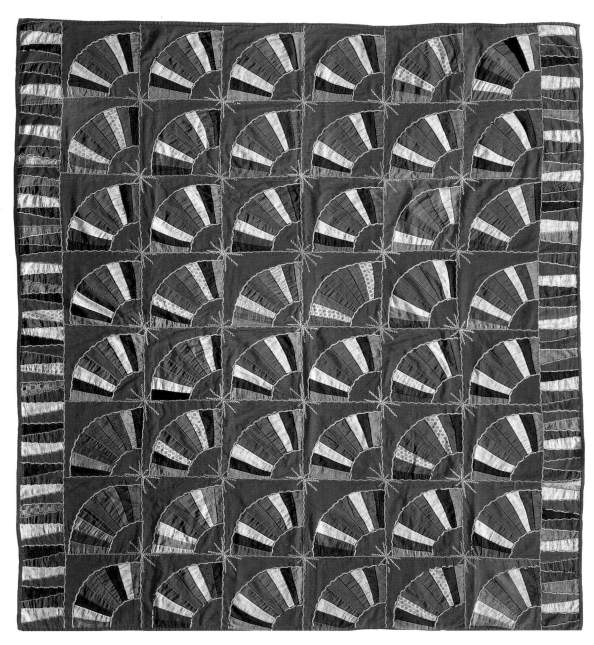

Fan, *the Shenandoah Valley (VA), c. 1880, cotton, 68 x 76½, made by Elizabeth Swope Suter, wife of well-known Mennonite potter Emanuel J. Suter, great-great-grandmother of the quilt's current owner, Scott Hamilton Suter.*

Elizabeth Swope Suter, wife of potter Emanuel Suter, likely made this quilt, perhaps with the help of her daughters.

She was an avid quiltmaker, making quilts for each of her 11 children who lived past infancy and piecing quilt tops for her 34 granddaughters (each was to quilt her own!).

Each Fan in this quilt is laid out similarly. A central red "spoke" is bordered on both sides by a blue spoke, with pairs of contrasting spokes moving out to the edge of each block. (The bottom right block is missing the red center piece. And it has only eight spokes, while all the other blocks have nine.)

The orderly piecing and the sober colors (including the clay-toned red of the background blocks) reflect Mennonite restraint.

The "Chinese Coins" side borders and the sprays of embroidery where the Fan blocks connect show this quiltmaker's ability to move beyond the ordinary.

Emanuel Suter, Mennonite Potter

The Emanuel and Elizabeth Suter Family, Saturday, August 1, 1896—Front: C. Charles, Virginia (Jennie), Emanuel, Elizabeth, Lillie, Reuben D., P. Swope. Back: John R., David I., Emanuel J., Eugene C., Perry G., Laura E.
Taken at the studio of Wm. Dean, Harrisonburg, VA.

Emanuel Suter (1833-1902) was a well established potter and highly regarded Mennonite church leader in the second half of the 19th century. He and his wife Elizabeth Swope reared 11 children to adulthood on a farm a few miles west of Harrisonburg, Virginia.

During the Civil War, the Suter family resettled for a few months near Harrisburg, Pennsylvania. Emanuel took a job with a potter there and gained new inspiration for his work.

During that time away from the Valley he began keeping a daily diary, a practice he continued for nearly 30 years.

When the family returned to the Valley, Suter built a new pottery shop and kiln. He named it New Erection Pottery, an operation that was to grow and flourish for 25 years.

An enterprising man, Suter built a new pottery on the edge of expanding Harrisonburg in early 1891. This venture was named the Harrisonburg Steam Pottery. Emanuel sold his interest there six years later. For his whole adult life, he had created and overseen the production of redware and gray stoneware in many functional forms—from crocks to tableware, from jugs to butter churns, from pitchers to teapots.

His work is sought after by collectors today. Recently two relatively small pieces were sold at an auction; one for $10,000; the other for $11,500.

From Emanuel Suter's diary—
Saturday, April 15, 1865

This forenoon we were sliping and painting ware, this afternoon I cam home in the 2 o'clock train. This morning we received the sad intelligence of the murder of A. Lincoln. It was cloudy and raining this afternoon.

Wednesday, September 26, 1894

Today Eugene and I drilled wheat in the 12 acre field next to Showalters we finished that field this evening Perry harrowed until dinner. then this afternoon he went to town after a load of fertilizer. The girls have a quilt in the frame and they are quilting it. Fannie Suter was helping them this afternoon.

Suter Pottery: Three pieces of redware made by well-known Mennonite potter, Emanuel Suter (1833-1902).

Front left—a love feast bowl, used for serving soup at Church of the Brethren congregational love feasts. The bowl is stamped "E. Suter."

Rear—a crock. Notice the potter's mark near the top: 1/2.

Front right—a bank. Suter made these banks to be broken when they were full.

Pottery from the collection of Beverley and Jeffrey S. Evans.

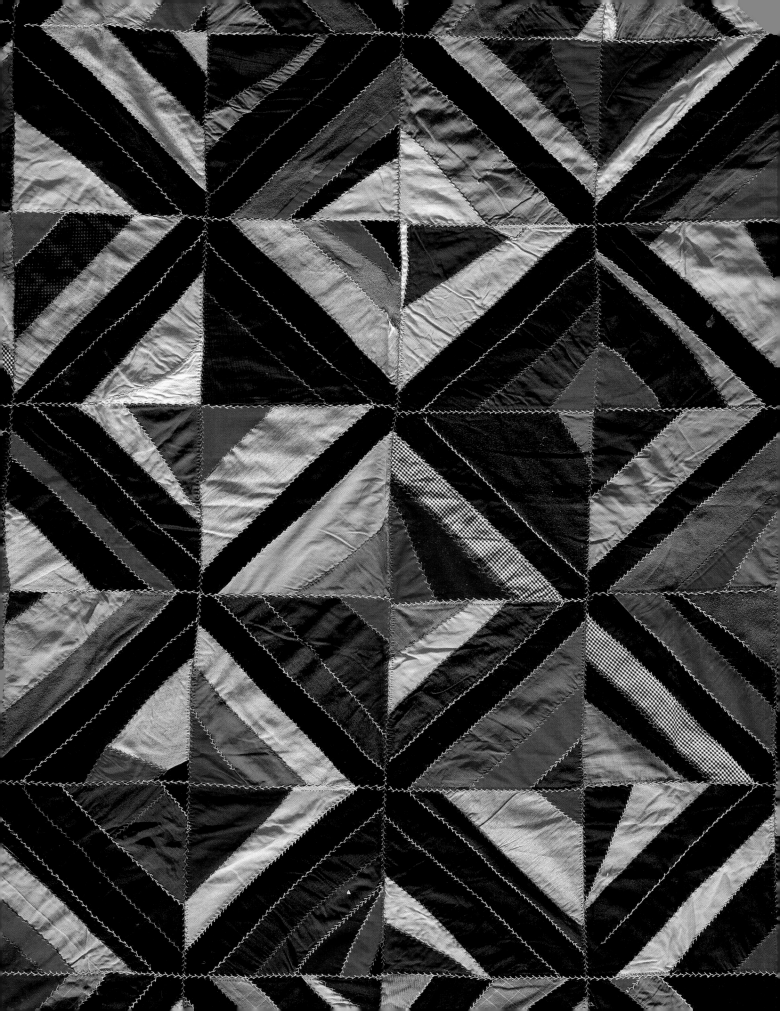

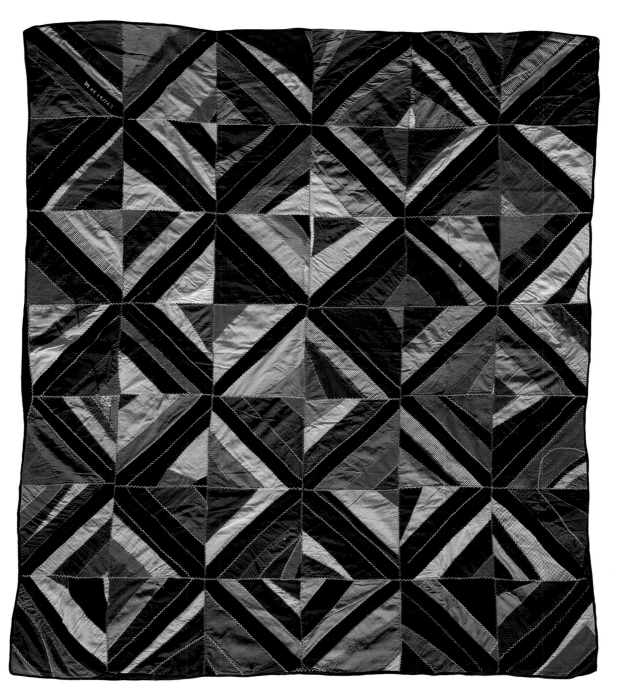

Log Cabin / Roman Stripe, *the Shenandoah Valley (VA), May 19, 1927, cotton and wool coat and dress fabrics, 69¹⁄₂ x 79, made either by Emma Martin Rhodes or her daughter, Mary Rhodes Burkholder (members of the Old Order Mennonites), grandmother and mother of the quilt s current owners, Grace, Oliver, and Harry Burkholder.*

Sometimes subtle colors and precise piecing give way to flair and a touch of mayhem.

Did the quiltmaker have a guiding design? Most of the blocks are made up of diagonal strips, finished with triangles in two opposite corners. The blocks are assembled to create a Log Cabin / Roman Stripe effect.

Here and there a block is patched to make it square, but the repair effort is never hidden. The addition is usually made of bright, contrasting fabric.

The presence of a central strip of black, navy, or brown in each block steadies the quilt over all.

Pinwheels, *the Shenandoah Valley (VA), c. 1925, cotton, 73 x 75, made by Mary Rhodes Burkholder (a member of the Old Order Mennonites), mother of the current owners, Grace, Oliver, and Harry Burkholder.*

A quilt of utter simplicity, yet full of ringing charm.

The sharp points of the pinwheel triangles receive reinforcement from the "soft" triangles in the sawtooth border surrounding the central field.

The weaving vine of quilting in the creamy inner border is a gentle foil to the fine crosshatching covering the rest of the quilt.

Mary made this quilt before her wedding, perhaps in anticipation of her marriage and children, to whom the quilt was eventually given.

Musical Scores and Singing Schools

The Mennonites of the Shenandoah Valley loved music, but that did not make them unique Mennonites. Rather, they are stand-outs in music because of the bold leadership—both official and unofficial—they experienced. Until the mid-1800s, the Valley churches sang the *Ausbund* texts, a German language songbook without musical scores, used widely by Amish and Mennonites, first in Europe and then in North America.

Joseph and Christian Funk, music lovers from the Valley's Northern District, were active congregational song leaders. Joseph had begun compiling hymnals as early as 1816. In the 1840s, Virginia Conference appointed him, along with David Hartman and Joseph Wenger, to select hymns for an *English*-language hymnal. They

compiled *A Selection of Psalms, Hymns, and Spiritual Songs;* the collection was published in 1847, designed as a companion volume to Funk's *Genuine Church Music,* a book of tunes.

This rare move by the Conference was followed by its officially sanctioning singing schools in 1860. In those popular gatherings, Mennonites were taught how to sing in three- and four-part harmony.

A sizable segment of the Conference subscribed to the use of English, singing in harmony, and organizing Sunday schools. Another portion of the Mennonites in the Valley believed there was danger in this direction, that change would tempt members away from humility and toward the loss of a faithful community.

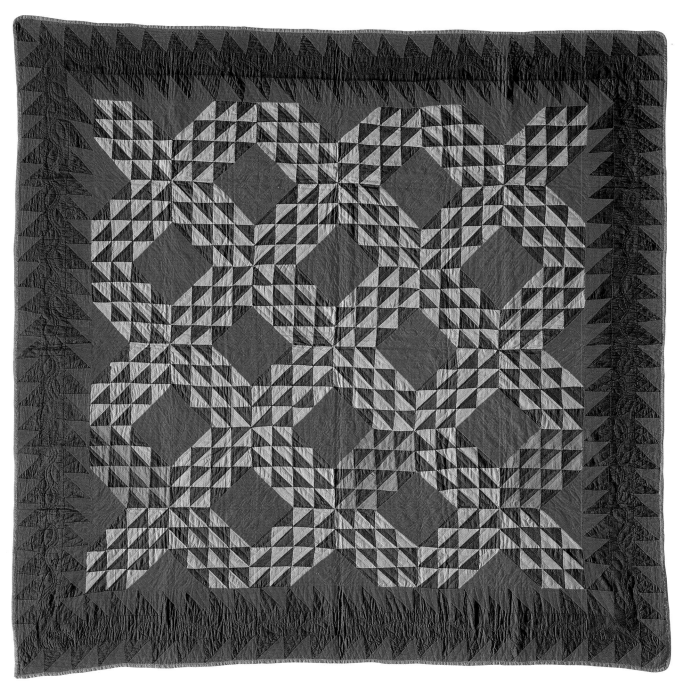

Ocean Waves, *the Shenandoah Valley (VA), c. 1920s, cotton, 69½ x 71, made by Emma Martin Rhodes (a member of the Old Order Mennonites), grandmother of the current owners, Grace, Oliver, and Harry Burkholder.*

In this Ocean Waves quilt, the plain, unpieced red blocks move into the foreground and the pieced triangles seem to recede. Not only are the small pink and green triangles reticent in color, they are arranged in clusters around the red squares, rather than establishing strong diagonal paths across the face of the quilt.

The powerful Flying Geese border vies for attention with the plain red blocks in the interior, creating an interplay with pleasing tension. Here again, as she did on her Wishing Ring quilt (page 61), Emma gave a different tilt to the triangles along the top border, producing a kind of lightning effect.

Grandmother's Flower Garden, *the Shenandoah Valley (VA), 1934, cotton, 71 x 81, made by Margaret Shank (a member of Pike Mennonite Church), currently owned by Miriam S. Shenk.*

By choosing colors of nearly equal value, Margaret produced a quilt that is primarily a wash of pink. The flowers dominate the paths of white between them.
Partial flowers fill up the spaces along the sides of the interior; half-flowers the top and bottom edges.
The pink ring of petals in each flower is strengthened by the outer peach borders.
The two borders gave Margaret a chance to bring quilted plumes and hearts to her work, a significant addition to the standard outline quilting in the flower patches. (Some Flower Garden quilts have no borders, finishing instead with a jagged edge.)

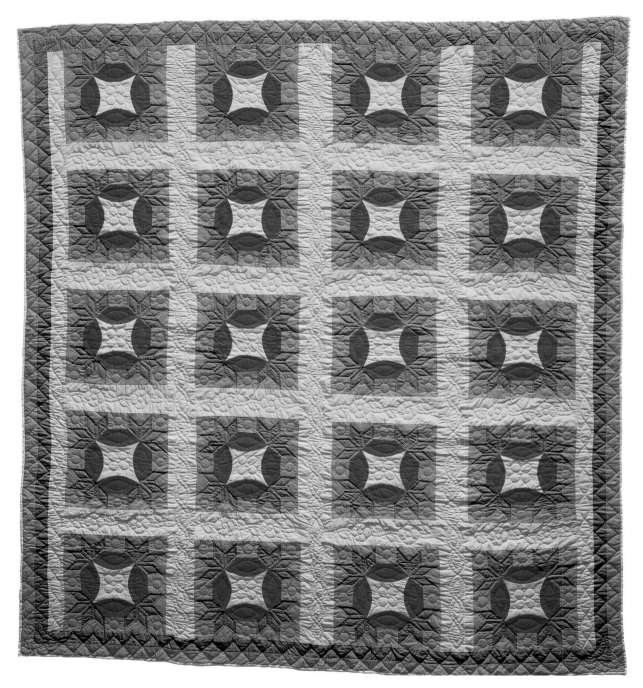

Old-Fashioned Star, *the Shenandoah Valley (VA), 1935, cotton, 75 x 82, made by Emma Martin Rhodes (a member of the Old Order Mennonites) for her grandson Oliver Burkholder.*

Emma Martin Rhodes may have sensed that her grandson Oliver Burkholder might not have been drawn to or impressed by quilts. (Boys in this rural Mennonite world were trained to be good farmers and tradesmen.) Emma made a quilt no boy could ignore.

She also cut no corners in her workmanship. The concave yellow patches and their partner convex red pieces lie flat and hold their shape; the teal diamonds are sharp and crisp. The pink plays a background role, kept there by the wildly yellow sashing.

Emma chose no fussy quilt designs. Instead she stitched a chain, circles, and diamonds, and a flat, stylized flower.

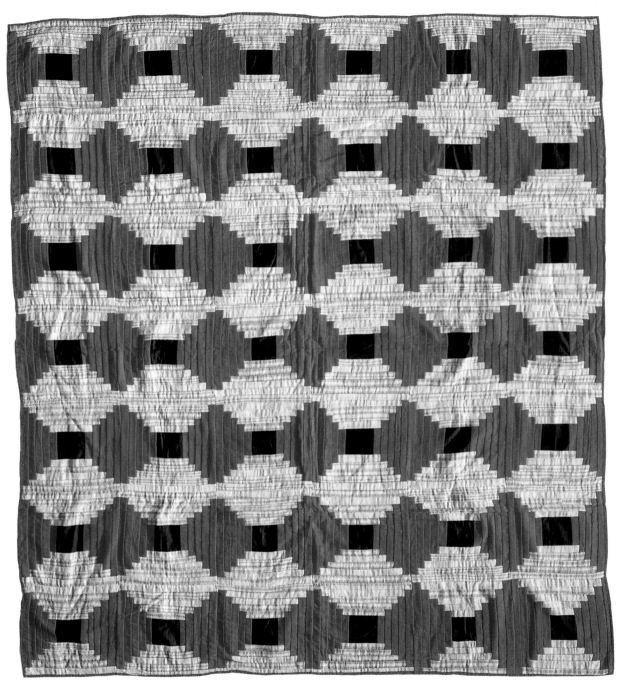

Log Cabin / Courthouse Steps, *the Shenandoah Valley (VA), c. 1900, cotton, 63½ x 73½, made by Hannah and Mary Elizabeth (Molly) Brenneman, members of the Mt. Carmel Church at Fulks Run and great-aunts of the current owner.*

    A measured and stately quilt. Each block is made up of three fabrics—an unusually large black center; on two of its sides lie five black-and-white striped logs; on its other two sides lie five red longs. A thin red binding frames the quilt, which has no other borders.
    Hannah and Mary Elizabeth (Molly) Brenneman were single sisters who shared a home and a love of quiltmaking. Hannah liked to travel; Molly preferred to stay home and look after the house.

The Shenandoah Valley holds its breathless beauty yet today.

Variable Star Album, *the Big Valley (PA), 1930, cotton sateen, 70 x 70, private collection.*

    Each of the 16 blocks in this Album quilt is a pieced star. Fifteen of the blocks present the same star pattern; the central square of each is pieced in a different design, however.

    The sixteenth patch is a greater variation (see the upper right corner). It has only six points; all the others have eight. It is composed entirely of diamond-shaped pieces, while the others are a series of triangles and squares.

    This quiltmaker found a way to stay within her faith community, yet still express her creative color and design energies. The reverse side of the quilt is a Bars pattern, far simpler, less showy, and so less threatening to a church group concerned with humility. The quiltmaker could decide which side to turn face up, depending upon who was visiting!

Index

Readings and Sources

Amish History

Good, Merle and Phyllis. *20 Most Asked Questions About the Amish and Mennonites.* Intercourse, PA: Good Books, 1995.

Hayes, A. Reed, Jr. *The Old Order Amish Mennonites of Pennsylvania.* Lewistown, PA: Mifflin County Historical Society, Inc., 1947.

Kauffman, S. Duane. *Mifflin County Amish and Mennonite Story 1791-1991.* Belleville, PA: Mifflin County Mennonite Historical Society, 1991.

Nolt, Steven M. *A History of the Amish.* Intercourse, PA: Good Books, 1992.

Renno, John R. *A Brief History of the Amish Church in Belleville,* n.p.

Scott, Stephen. *Plain Buggies.* Intercourse, PA: Good Books, 1998.

____. *Why Do They Dress That Way?* Intercourse, PA: Good Books, 1997.

Mennonite History

Brunk, Harry Anthony. *History of Mennonites in Virginia, 1727-1900, Volume I.* Harrisonburg, VA: H. A. Brunk, 1959.

Funk, Joseph and Sons. *The Harmonia Sacra, Twenty-fifth Edition.* Intercourse, PA: Good Books, 1993.

Good, Phyllis Pellman and Kate Good. *Mennonite Recipes from the Shenandoah Valley.* Intercourse, PA: Good Books, 1999.

Hartman, Peter S. *Reminiscences of the Civil War.* Lancaster, PA: Eastern Mennonite Associated Libraries and Archives, 1964.

Horst, Samuel. *Mennonites in the Confederacy: A Study in Civil War Pacifism.* Scottdale, PA: Herald Press, 1967.

Kaufman, Stanley A. *Heatwole and Suter Pottery.* Harrisonburg, VA: Eastern Mennonite College, 1978.

MacMaster, Richard K. *Land, Piety, Peoplehood.* Scottdale, PA: Herald Press, 1985.

Scott, Stephen. *An Introduction to Old Order and Conservative Mennonite Groups.* Intercourse, PA: Good Books, 1996.

Amish and Mennonite Quilts

Granick, Eve Wheatcroft. *The Amish Quilt.* Intercourse, PA: Good Books, 1989.

Hayes, Connie and Evelyn Gleason. "Nebraska Quilts; The Discovery of a Distinctive Style of Amish Quilts," *Antique Collecting 2,* no. 8 (January 1979), 21-28.

Pellman, Rachel and Kenneth. *A Treasury of Amish Quilts.* Intercourse, PA: Good Books, 1998.

____. *A Treasury of Mennonite Quilts.* Intercourse, PA: Good Books, 1992.

____. *The World of Amish Quilts.* Intercourse, PA: Good Books, 1998.

About the Author

Phyllis Pellman Good has explored and written extensively about Amish and Mennonite faith and culture. She is co-author (with her husband Merle) of *20 Most Asked Questions About the Amish and Mennonites* and co-editor (also with Merle) of the series of books *What Mennonites Are Thinking, 1998, 1999,* and *2000.* Her other books include *Perils of Professionalism, A Mennonite Woman's Life, Mennonite Recipes from the Shenandoah Valley* (with her daughter Kate), *The Best of Amish Cooking, The Best of Mennonite Fellowship Meals, Christmas Ideas for Families* (with Merle), and a children's book, *Plain Pig's ABC's: A Day on Plain Pig's Amish Farm.*

Good is curator of The People's Place Quilt Museum, located in the village of Intercourse (Lancaster County), Pennsylvania. The Museum specializes in exhibiting changing shows of antique Amish and Mennonite quilts, and has enjoyed critical acclaim from national publications.

Good is General Manager of the historic Old Country Store in the original part of the village of Intercourse. The Old Country Store has been chosen as one of the "10 best quilt shops in America" by Better Homes and Gardens *Quilt Sampler.*

Phyllis and Merle Good are also co-directors of The People's Place (also in Intercourse), an educational and heritage center dedicated to interpreting Amish and Mennonite beliefs and practices.